Norf

A DOG WALKER'S GUIDE

Angela Youngman

COUNTRYSIDE BOOKS
NEWBURY BERKSHIRE

First published 2014
© Angela Youngman 2014
Reprinted 2016, 2018

COUNTRYSIDE BOOKS
3 Catherine Road
Newbury, Berkshire

To view our complete range of books,
please visit us at
www.countrysidebooks.co.uk

ISBN 978 1 84674 319 1

Cover photograph supplied by Roger Evans

Designed by Peter Davies, Nautilus Design
Produced through The Letterworks Ltd., Reading
Typeset by KT Designs, Newton-le-Willows
Printed by The Holywell Press, Oxford

Contents

Walk

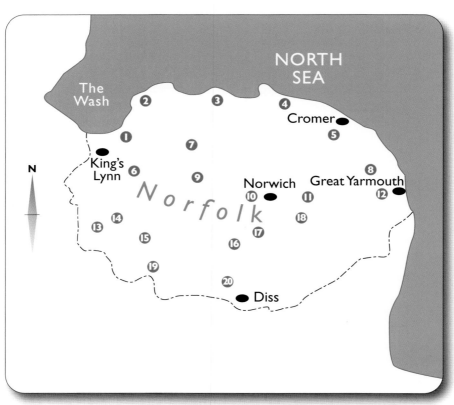

Area map showing location of the walks.

INTRODUCTION

Norfolk is a county of contrasting landscapes – the watery setting of the Broads with its beautiful lakes and rivers; hills and gently rolling fields; sandy heaths, pine forests and the wide expanse of fenland where the horizon stretches uninterrupted for miles. Then there is the coastline with its miles of beaches, cliffs, sand dunes and marshes offering plenty of room to run and play. Historical sites and links add extra interest; the variety is endless. Not surprisingly, such an area offers fantastic walking opportunities – especially if you are a dog owner!

Researching this book was great fun for everyone involved, especially the hardworking paws of the English cocker spaniels Freddie and Melodie and the terrier Scamp. All the walks provide lots of opportunities to explore and investigate making them perfect for curious dogs. Different walks provide added stimulation, as well as exercise and play.

Some areas such as Thetford Forest, Sandringham and the Wells to Holkham beach walk are good for encouraging dog socialization as these are locations where other dogs are most likely to be present. We met many dogs and dog owners along the way, all of whom proved helpful and informative. My thanks to everyone (and their dogs) who helped make this so much fun.

Each walk includes details on local vets, where to park and refreshments. Bear in mind that things can change and free parking can suddenly become fee paying. Likewise, pubs and cafés may close or change hands, so it is worth checking the current status regarding opening times. At the time of writing, all the venues listed were dog friendly.

Angela Youngman

. . . .

PUBLISHER'S NOTE

We hope that you obtain considerable enjoyment from this book; great care has been taken in its preparation. Although at the time of publication all routes followed public rights of way or permitted paths, diversion orders can be made and permissions withdrawn.

We cannot, of course, be held responsible for such diversion orders and any inaccuracies in the text which result from these or any other changes to the routes nor any damage which might result from walkers trespassing on private property. We are anxious though that all details covering the walks are kept up to date and would therefore welcome information from readers which would be relevant to future editions.

The simple sketch maps that accompany the walks in this book are based on notes made by the author whilst checking out the routes on the ground. They are designed to show you how to reach the start, to point out the main features of the overall circuit and they contain a progression of numbers that relate to the paragraphs of the text.

However, for the benefit of a proper map, we do recommend that you purchase the relevant Ordnance Survey sheet covering your walk. The Ordnance Survey maps are widely available, especially through booksellers and local newsagents.

. . . .

Acknowledgements: The publishers would like to thank Liz Moynihan and Roger Hacon for their help in preparing this book.

ADVICE FOR DOG WALKERS

'The countryside is a great place to exercise dogs but it is every owner's duty to make sure their dog is not a danger or nuisance to farm animals, wildlife or other people' (taken from the Countryside Code, available on Natural England's website (www.naturalengland.org.uk/ourwork/enjoying/countrysidecode).

With a large open coastline, heaths, fields and woods; Norfolk is a wonderful place for dogs and their owners to enjoy the countryside. It is a rural county where agriculture is predominant. Most of the fields are used for growing crops, but livestock such as horses, cattle, sheep and pigs are also present. Geese and turkeys may be found in places. Ground-nesting birds may be present in the heathlands and around the dunes. Rabbits are very much in evidence within many of the fields and woods. Muntjac deer do roam freely throughout the county.

All of these animals and birds are vulnerable to dogs. This includes dogs who are just having fun and enjoying a run even if they are not obviously hurting or chasing wildlife. Wildlife and farm animals do not know the difference. It is important to keep dogs close or on a lead during the March to July nesting season. Dogs should also be kept on leads during visits to beaches used by packs of breeding seals during the period December-March. Other restrictions on access to beaches may exist during the summer period.

Please observe any notices that you see en route requesting dogs to be kept on leads. Such notices are put up for the safety of all users of the countryside.

Sheep and lambs usually move away from dogs. But be aware that some dogs have a natural tendency to enter fields by any method possible in order to give chase. As a dog owner, you need to prevent this. It can cause sheep to abort their lambs, and farmers are allowed by law to shoot any dog worrying livestock. If you see sheep in a field, put your dog on a lead immediately.

Several walks border on rivers, streams or broads with no fencing. These are often deep and can be full of reeds, mud and weeds so are not suitable for swimming by people or dogs.

Cattle and horses are naturally inquisitive and may follow you across a field. This can be scary, especially if an entire herd decides to follow you. Just continue walking steadily and do not let your dog near the cattle.

Beware of rabbit holes. These are found in large numbers throughout many of the walks. Some dogs thoroughly enjoy the opportunity to chase a rabbit, and will follow them down a hole – and get stuck. This may result in you having to dig out the dog! Or even worse, lose them as the chase can cover long distances.

Always take bags to remove dog poo, especially in car parks, picnic areas, roads and paths. If there are no dog bins available; the usual advice is to take it home with you. Never leave bagged poo in the countryside – it will not degrade naturally. The plastic litters the countryside and can cause problems for wildlife who may think it is food and try to eat it.

Seasonal Canine Disease has occurred in Norfolk. The symptoms include diarrhea and vomiting which can be severe and appear about 24 to 48 hours after being infected. The exact cause is unknown. Suggestions have included mites, virus and bacteria. The Animal Health Centre in Newmarket is investigating the disease. In depth study areas exist nationwide, but in Norfolk the two areas under study are Sandringham and Thetford. Although it is rare, it can occur during the autumn usually after walks in woodland. The advice is to reduce the risk of encountering any infection by keeping dogs on leads for a couple of months during the autumn, especially when walking in woodland areas. If your dog should show any symptoms, then take it to a vet as quickly as possible.

Ticks are common in most woodland and countryside areas from spring through to autumn. These blood sucking parasites feed off livestock until bloated, then drop off and cling to bracken and bushes. They can attach themselves to a dog's fur when it runs through the undergrowth. People can attract them too, especially on exposed legs and arms. Bites may not be felt until later when the skin can become infected and sore. A further problem is caused by the fact that ticks can cause Lyme Disease - a serious illness that can affect both humans and dogs. This disease has flu-like symptoms but can result in complications if it is not treated by medical practitioners.

Avoid ticks as much as possible by wearing long sleeved tops, shoes rather than sandals and long trousers tucked into your socks. Light coloured clothing will help show up any ticks that do appear.

If a tick does attach itself, you need to remove it as quickly as possible. This reduces the chance of any disease being transmitted. It is possible to buy special removal devices, but you can use tweezers or in some cases, fingernails. To remove a tick, push the tweezers or fingernails as far as possible under the tick's body close to the skin. Then pull straight out, without squeezing. Do not twist or simply pull the tick away. This can do more harm than good as it will merely remove the body of the tick. The head and mouth may remain in the skin. The possibility of infection will remain as long as the head or body are present.

Further sources of information on dog walking in Norfolk
http://www.north-norfolk.gov.uk/tasks/environmental-protection/where-you-can-cant-take-your-dog. This site deals with orders restricting dog access to beaches in north Norfolk.
http://www.forestry.gov.uk/forestry/beeh-9vkj6d. This site provides advice on managing dogs in woodlands and ensuring that the needs of others are maintained.

1

Sandringham

Sandringham House is set in 24 acres of stunning gardens.

Here is a walk with Royal connections as Sandringham is the Queen's Norfolk home. It is where she and other members of the Royal Family come to celebrate Christmas and New Year. It was built in 1870 by the then Prince and Princess of Wales (later King Edward VII and Queen Alexandra), and was once described as, 'the most comfortable house in England'. The house, museum and garden are open whenever members of the Royal Family are not in residence, and they make Sandringham one of the most popular destinations for visitors to East Anglia.

The adjacent country park is open all year round, as is the visitor centre. It provides a wonderful location for walking dogs. Friendly, relaxing and very accessible, the woodland walks are always a pleasure. No matter what the time of year, the paths are firm and the walking is good. Although it can get very popular in summer, the site is so large that you do not realise there are so many people around. It is possible to walk some distance before meeting anyone and the woods are very tranquil.

Throughout the woodland, Corsican and Scots pine are much in evidence as are oak, sweet chestnut and graceful birch trees. With this mix of deciduous and evergreen trees, the woodland provides plenty of dappled shade in the summer to keep even the most active dog cool. As well as the waymarked routes, there are plenty of bark paths offering opportunities to explore quiet corners of the estate. Please note, however, that dogs are not allowed in the gardens of Sandringham House, only in the country park.

Terrain

Woodland bark and wide grassy paths, some of which run alongside concrete roads enabling walkers to avoid traffic. Most of the route is flat, although there is a steeper gradient towards the end of the walk. There are some estate roads and minor B roads crossing the estate, but it is possible to avoid these if you want.

Where to park

Main free large all-weather parking by the visitor centre. **OS map:** Landranger 132 North West Norfolk.

How to get there

Sandringham is situated 6 miles north-east of King's Lynn. The estate is signposted from both the A148 Fakenham road and the A149 Hunstanton road. Look out for the brown tourist sign followed by P which indicates the main car park.

Nearest refreshments

Café, picnic area, shops and toilets can be found in the visitor centre. There is an extensive grassed area adjacent to the picnic area where dogs can play and run (☎ 01485 544548).

Dog factors
. . . .

Distance: 2 miles.
Road walking: The walk involves crossing minor roads, and walking along an estate road which has a wide grassy road edge.
Livestock: None.
Stiles: None.
Nearest vets: Sunnyside Veterinary Clinic, Hall Farm, Church Lane, Roydon, King's Lynn PE32 1AR. ☎ 01485 600022.

Norfolk – A Dog Walker's Guide

The Walk

. . . .

1 From the front of the visitor centre, turn right along a sandy path and head for the children's playground.

2 Look for the wooden statue of a bear (blue and yellow markers). This marks the start of the woodland walks. Walk straight ahead past the pretty woodland sculptures – look carefully at the bird perched high on a tree trunk and you will see a door at the bottom!

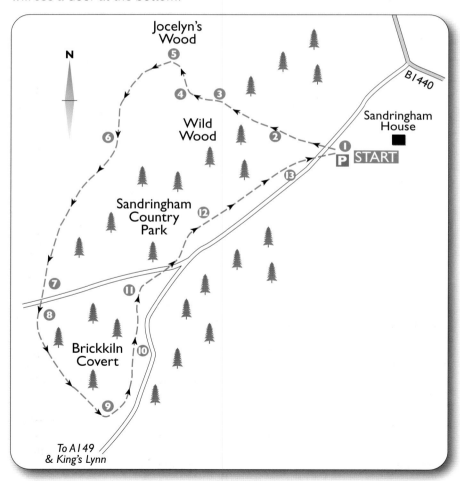

3 At the junction of two tracks, beside some tall rhododendrons, take the left-hand turning indicated by a **blue marker**.

4 Walk only a short distance down this track and look for a turning to the right, just before a blue marker on a tree on the left. This leads onto a narrower bark path. Follow the path straight ahead through stands of holly and deciduous trees. Continue into a more open glade and go ahead through bushes and onto a concrete road.

5 Turn left past the rhododendron bushes. The path is now quite wide with grassy areas on either side of a concrete estate road. Cars are sometimes parked on the grass at the side of the road. This path is part of a scenic drive through the park.

6 Keep walking ahead for some distance. The terrain is firm and comfortable to walk on as you can choose either the grassy verge or the concrete roadway. Ignore all side paths including the blue arrowed path to the left (opposite this a short way to the right is a viewing platform with a lovely view to the distant sea).

7 Go through the iron gates marked with an **ER symbol**. The path leads down to a public minor road. Cross with care, and directly opposite you will see a **yellow marker** on a post. This marks the entrance to the path.

8 Walk ahead for some distance along this pleasant path. Take care as some large tree roots stick up from the ground in places. This section of the woodland is very much composed of native trees such as silver birch and Scots pine.

9 At the end of the track you will see a road straight ahead. Just before the road there is a grassy area with two large silver birch trees to the left-hand side. Turn left onto the grassy, bark path which leads slightly uphill. The path changes from grass to purely pine needles and bark.

10 At the top of the small hill, look for a row of low tree trunks across the path. Almost immediately afterwards, the path ahead forks. Take the left-hand path. This path leads further into the woodland before opening onto a wide drove.

11 Turn right and walk down the drove. This leads to a Y junction with minor roads on either side. There is a brick wall alongside the right-hand road. Bear left at the Y junction and cross over the road heading for the woodland, keeping the wall directly behind you. Aim for the **yellow marker** post.

12 The path leads into the woodland. About a minute further on, there is a junction with another path. Turn right and follow the path through the wood. This path runs roughly adjacent to the road which can be heard in the distance, but not seen. There's a dog waste container alongside this path. The path ends opposite a sign saying 'Welcome to Sandringham'. Return to the visitor centre across the grass slightly to the left.

Woodland paths for your dog to explore.

2

Holme-next-the-Sea

Holme sits within the North Norfolk Heritage coast.

This walk explores a quiet riverside, peaceful village streets and a beautiful coastline. Holme-next-the-Sea is a small village not far from the seaside resort of Hunstanton. A pretty village with a stunning beach, it does not attract the large crowds that you find in its bigger neighbour. If your dog loves seaweed there is plenty to play in. All along the beach there are massive clumps of seaweed left high on the strand line, along with masses upon masses of seashells.

The path takes you by the River Hun where swans and ducks can frequently be seen swimming. It is a pretty river with good views across the surrounding countryside, plus an adjacent golf course which has to be crossed twice during the walk. Large numbers of golf balls litter the course – but there is a fence preventing dogs from entering and collecting them.

The North Norfolk coast is definitely one of the glories of the county. The sand is firm and clean, and a brisk breeze from the North Sea is very common. The sound of the waves is never far away as they break across the edge of the beach. Deep lagoons separated by sand dunes dot the beach, which can quickly become covered in sea water when the tide comes rushing in.

Ideal for a brisk coastal walk, this is an area with much to offer, see and do while still enjoying the peace and tranquillity of the Norfolk countryside.

Norfolk – A Dog Walker's Guide

Dog factors

Distance: 4 miles (5 miles for the longer walk)
Road walking: A short distance on village roads without pavements.
Livestock: None.
Stiles: None.
Off lead: On beach.
Nearest vets: Medivet, 95 Westgate, Hunstanton PE36 5EP.
☎ 01485 535950.

Terrain

Beach, grassy paths which can get quite narrow; both pavement and unpaved roads.

Where to park

On entering Holme-next-the-Sea drive straight through the village and head for the beach. There is a large car park at the end of the road. There is a small charge during busy periods. There are toilets opposite the car park. **OS map:** Landranger 132 North West Norfolk (GR 697438).

How to get there

Holme-next-the-Sea is off the A149 coast road and just east of Hunstanton.

Nearest refreshments

There is a refreshment kiosk in the car park in high summer. Alternatively, try the White Horse pub, Kirkgate Street, Holme-next-the-Sea. (☎ 01485 525512).

The Walk

1 Leave the car park by the main entrance and turn left. Walk down the road a short distance. Just after passing a caravan site – and before you reach the bridge – there is a footpath to the right highlighted by a **yellow waymarker**. Take this path and walk straight ahead. It leads behind the caravan site to a small bridge.

2 Cross the bridge and walk onwards along the river bank. The path can get a bit muddy and uneven. The river is quite deep and fast moving, edged with reeds. Swans and ducks are frequently seen swimming on the river. There is a golf course on the other side of the path.

③ Eventually the path veers to the right, following the route of a small stream. The path steadily gets narrower. Eventually the stream peters out into a muddy ditch. At this point, the path reaches a junction with a road.

④ Turn right and follow the road towards the **clubhouse**. Turn right at the permitted path across the golf course. Walk straight ahead towards the **beach huts** in the distance.

⑤ When you reach the beach huts, there is a choice of paths. You can either turn right and follow the coastal path behind the beach huts along the top of the sand dunes, or scramble up the dunes and down onto the beach.

Take care if you choose the beach route. Stay close to the dunes and do not venture far out onto the beach. There are deep lagoons separated by stretches of sand. The tide can come in very fast leaving walkers marooned on the sandbanks, awaiting rescue by the inshore lifeboat.

⑥ Turn right and walk along the strand line where there are frequently large heaps of seaweed and shells. Keep walking along the beach until you reach a pathway leading up onto the dunes near a little shed. Take this pathway.

⑦ Having climbed up the dunes, you will then be on the **coastal pathway**. Turn left and walk on. This path leads away from the beach across the salt marshes.

⑧ When you reach a signpost and a No Through Road sign, there is a choice of paths. Turn right and cross the golf course with care to reach the car park. Watch out for golfers

Racing along the dunes.

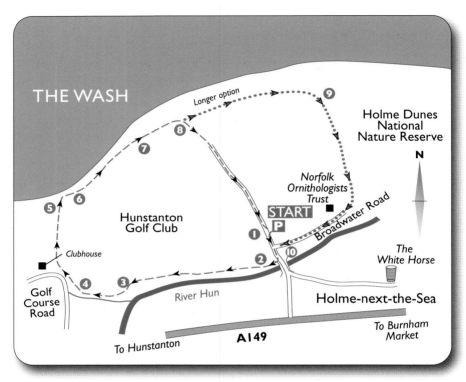

about to take a shot – the balls may come in your direction.

For a longer walk, turn left and carry on walking along the path through the salt marsh. It passes the edge of the golf course before going through an area of scrub land. The wide path becomes much more solid, smooth and well made.

9 Look for a house with a tall watchtower in the garden. Just after this house, there is a rough path leading down to a tarmac road. Take this turning. Once on the road, turn right and follow the quiet private road past the **Norfolk Wildlife Trust cabin** and the entrance to the **Norfolk Ornithology Nature Reserve**. Continue walking along the road, past the **watchtower** used by members of the Norfolk Ornithology Trust as a bird hide. There are seats along the road where you can relax for a few minutes in a grassy area.

10 At the end of the road, turn right and walk back along the pavement to the car park.

3

Wells and Holkham

A row of beach huts at Wells.

This is definitely one of **Freddie, Melodie and Scamp's** all time favourite walks and it is easy to see why as it involves a wonderful mix of sea, sand and forest. There is plenty of room to play, chase and run to their hearts' content. There are always other dogs to greet and lots of smells, dunes and water to investigate. Wide expanses of golden sands are interspersed with dunes and salt water lakes. The coastline changes from beach huts to sand dunes before becoming heavily lined with a mix of evergreen and deciduous trees.

Not surprisingly, this area is very popular during the summer, as visitors are attracted by the long expanses of golden sand. The sea goes out quite a long way and when the tide is out, it can be over fifteen minutes walk from the coastline to the edge of the sea. The beach at Holkham Gap has featured in films such as *Shakespeare in Love* in which actress Gwyneth Paltrow was shown walking up the beach at the end of the film.

A good all-year-round walk, it makes for a fun experience for everyone. The stimulating sea breezes definitely keep you awake and alert, while the sandy beach is easy on the feet.

Terrain

Sand and bark paths – usually quite dry, but wellies may be needed in winter. The tide can come in very swiftly. For safety, keep to the area near to the coastal dunes. It is easy to get stranded in the outlying areas.

Where to park

There is a public car park with toilets on Beach Road in Wells-next-the-Sea. It has a small charge. **OS map:** Landranger 132 North West Norfolk (GR 914455).

How to get there

Take the A149 coast road (Hunstanton to Cromer) to Wells-next-the-Sea. Drive into Wells and take the turning marked Beach Road at the side of the quay. This leads past the Wells Harbour Railway. At the far end of the road, the car park can be seen on the left.

Nearest refreshments

The Beach Café by the car park is extremely dog friendly – it even has its 'Beach Café Dog of the Year' competition and a K9 club with plenty of water bowls and dog biscuits (☎ 01328 713055).

Dog factors
. . . .

Distance: 3 miles.
Road walking: None.
Livestock: None.
Stiles: None.
Nearest vets: Glaven Veterinary Practice, Maryland, Polka Road, Wells-next-the-Sea NR23 1LY ☎ 01328 711022.

The Walk
. . . .

1 Leave the car park by the paths at the far end. There is a choice – take the steep steps straight onto the beach, or turn left through the gate for a gentler access. If turning left, walk through the gate and then along the path. It leads past a lake on the left-hand side.

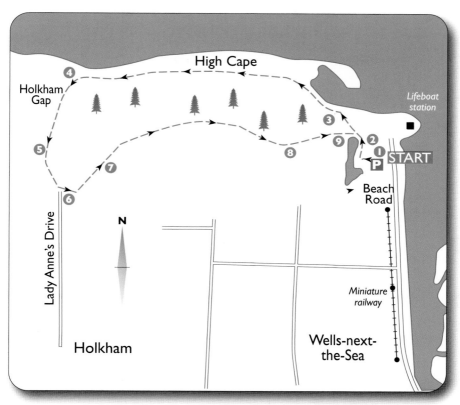

② At the signpost turn right. This path has a much gentler gradient leading to the beach. Pass between the beach huts onto the sand.

③ Turn left, and walk straight ahead. This is where there is another choice – you can walk along the top of the beach between the coastline and the first line of sand dunes, or go further out past the dunes and walk beside the sea. If you take the second route – beware of the tide. It can come in very quickly.

Whichever route is taken, walk straight ahead. There is no risk of getting lost – just keep the sea on your right and the coastline on your left!

The long stretches of sea pools found between the coast and the dunes are perfect for playing and paddling. Freddie, Melodie and Scamp loved splashing and chasing balls through the water and across the sands.

④ Continue walking straight ahead until the coastline begins to curve. In the centre of the curve, there is a short flight of steps leading up into the woods. This is known as **Holkham Gap**.

5 Follow the boardwalk straight ahead until you reach the entrance to **Lady Anne's Drive**.

6 Turn left just before the entrance to Lady Anne's Drive. This turning is marked by a **National Cycleway** signpost.

7 Walk ahead along the path. Made out of earth and stones, it can be a bit rough in places. There are fields belonging to the **Holkham estate** on the right, and woodland on the left. There is also a rush-filled ditch on the right – dogs keen on exploring it can get very muddy! The woodland starts as mainly evergreen with lots of Scots pine trees and slowly transforms into mixed woodland. There are many side paths into the woods which can be explored.

8 Eventually the path will fork. Take the left-hand path past the **Pinewoods Holiday Park**. There are lakes and streams along here which were very tempting for Freddie.

9 Keep walking ahead until you reach the lake. At the signpost, turn right and follow the path back to the car park.

Splashing about in the sea.

4

Salthouse Coastal Walk

An idyllic location for the Salthouse Dun Cow pub.

Whatever the weather, the salty air is invigorating. There are always lots of sea birds around, and not surprisingly the area here is popular with bird watchers. Dogs love the beach, shingle and the host of smells to be found on the grassy paths leading through the marshes, and this is an ideal walk for them.

This is a bleak and strangely beautiful landscape of beach, sea and salt marshes. From the shingle bank there are superb views, eastwards to Sheringham and west to Blakeney Point. Turn around and there is an incredible view of Salthouse set against a background of small hills.

A peaceful location that does not attract hordes of holiday makers, Salthouse has quite a history and elements of this can be seen throughout the walk. There are many reminders of the Second World War such as the concrete tank obstacles and gun emplacements. Even the name 'Salthouse' bears witness to a historic activity – the making of salt from sea water. The heath behind the village contains many prehistoric sites and the largest group of Bronze Age burial mounds in Norfolk.

Norfolk – A Dog Walker's Guide

Part of the route passes along the Norfolk Coast Path National Trail while the remainder are local paths across the salt marshes. These can get very wet and muddy, so strong footwear is essential.

Terrain
Grass, shingle and beach. It can be muddy with rough walking, especially in winter.

Where to park
Free parking is possible around the village green, which is immediately adjacent to the coast road. **OS map:** Landranger 133 North East Norfolk (GR 075438).

How to get there
Salthouse is on the A149 coast road, between Kelling and Cley-next-the-Sea.

Nearest refreshments
The picturesque Salthouse Dun Cow pub serves good food every day from 12 noon to 9 pm. ☎ 01263 740467 / NR25 7XA. Cookie's Crab Shop on The Green also serves hot and cold food every day. ☎ 01263 740352.

Dog factors

Distance: 2.5 miles.
Road walking: Approximately half a mile to and from the entrance and exit to the marshes.
Livestock: Cattle and horses graze freely on the marshes.
Stiles: None.
Off lead: On the beach.
Nearest vets: Miramar Veterinary Centre, 15 Weybourne Rd, Sheringham NR26 8HF. ☎ 01263 822293.

The Walk

1 After parking on **The Green**, go back to the main road and turn right. Cross the road and walk along the pavement for a few minutes.

2 Turn left at the public footpath sign which points across the marshes towards the sea in the far distance. The path leads across a deep ditch and onto the salt marshes. There are deep ditches on either side of the path.

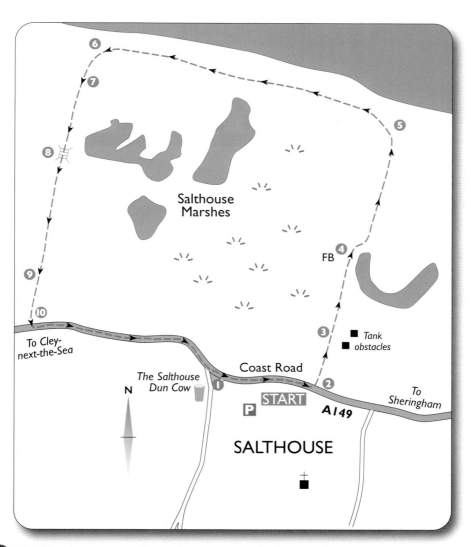

③ Walking along, you will pass large rectangular lumps of concrete in a field on the right-hand side. These formed part of the Second World War tank obstacles that were set up to prevent any German invasion. The flat North Norfolk beaches were regarded as potential location points for invasion forces. The beach itself was not opened to the public for several years after the war due to the need to clear mines from the area.

4 Just after passing a large oxbow lake on the right-hand side, there is a small bridge. Cross the bridge and follow the narrow path onto the shingle bank. The grassy path twists slightly to the right, before going straight ahead across the mud flats to the shingle, passing the remains of a Second World War gun emplacement on the right-hand side.

5 Turn left onto the high rise path at the top of the shingle bank. There are fantastic views out across the beach and the North Sea. The path is reasonably straight and firm. The shingle bank forms part of the sea defence network along this part of the coast. You can also scramble down the bank for a walk along the beach.

6 Walk along the top of the shingle bank until you reach the end of a large lake on your left. There is a pathway leading down towards a double dyke.

7 Follow the grassy path between the two dykes, heading towards **Salthouse** village. The dykes are deep, so keep to the path.

8 Cross the bridge with care. There is a hand rail on one side. The wooden planks can get slippery in wet weather.

9 Carry on walking up the grassy pathway. This can get very muddy at times, with uneven surfaces before it becomes much firmer and opens out into a flat area.

10 When you reach the road, turn left and follow the coastal road back towards **Salthouse**. There is no footpath, just a grass track. After passing the pub on the right, you'll see the village green.

Sandy paws and a waggy tail.

5

Felbrigg Woodland Walk

The Felbrigg estate sits within 520 acres of woods and parkland.

This **gentle and relaxing walk** takes you through well established, mainly deciduous woodland plus some open parkland. The bark paths are a delight to walk on, easy on the feet and paws. Wide droves narrow into small, secluded paths, before suddenly opening out into pretty clearings. In the autumn it is a spectacular sight with trees covered in yellow, gold and orange leaves. Wildlife is present, but was not much in evidence when we did the walk. There were definitely many enticing smells for Freddie and Melodie. The final stretch of the walk through the fields is slightly uphill, and offers extremely good views of the house and grounds.

The woodland is extensive, covering around 380 acres. It is well maintained and accessible at all times of the year. There are thousands of oaks, beeches and sycamore trees including some intriguing gnarled, older specimens reminiscent of *The Lord of the Rings*.

Felbrigg Hall has a large and substantial estate in the care of the National Trust and is one of the finest country houses in East Anglia. It occupies a commanding position between Sheringham and Holt, yet is well screened by woodland from the nearby main roads. The splendid 17th-century Hall was built in the Jacobean style, which makes the interior something of a surprise. You expect wooden panelling and dark rooms; instead there is lots of brightly painted Georgian décor and light coloured furniture reflecting the remodelling that took place during the 19th century. The gardens are interesting and well kept.

Terrain

Bark paths and fields. Easy walking along woodland paths. Only one small estate road has to be crossed. Much of the route is marked by red waymakers. Dogs do not have to be kept on leads, although it is recommended for the final part of the walk if there are cattle in the fields.

Where to park

There is a large car park on site which is free of charge to National Trust members; non-members pay a small charge.

How to get there

Felbrigg is situated in North Norfolk, just off the A140 Cromer to Norwich Road. Take the turning in Roughton marked Felbrigg/Sheringham. It can also be reached from the A148 Cromer to Holt road. **OS map:** Landranger 133 North East Norfolk (GR 193394 / NR11 8PR).

Dog factors

Distance: 4 miles.
Road walking: An estate road has to be crossed at one point, but this is a very quiet road used as an exit from the estate.
Livestock: Sheep or cattle may be in the fields at the end of the walk.
Stiles: None.
Off lead: Yes.
Nearest vets: Miramar Veterinary Centre, 15 Weybourne Rd, Sheringham NR26 8HF. ☎ 01263 822293.

Nearest refreshments

There is a picnic area at Felbrigg Hall visitor centre and dogs are allowed outside the Felbrigg Hall tearoom. Alternatively, try the Squire's Pantry for light meals and snacks. ☎ 01263 837444.

The Walk

. . . .

① From the car park, walk towards the house. As you pass through the hedged gateway, turn to your right and take the wide path ahead of you.

② Follow the path almost up to a walled enclosure, which is closed to the public.

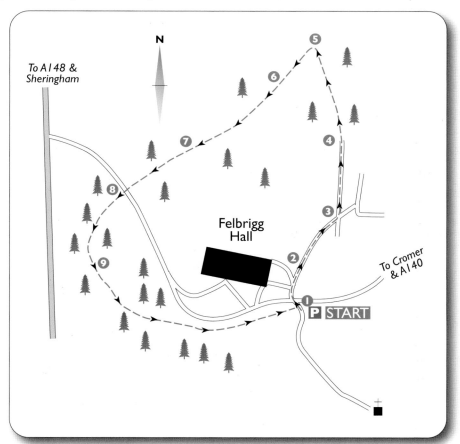

Exploring a woodland trail.

3 Turn to the left and follow the path into the woodland. Trees slowly close up around the path, but it is never claustrophobic. Sounds become deadened as the surface of the path becomes a deep layer of bark.

4 Keep following this path. It is a fairly straight path with the occasional slight bends as it meanders round some particularly wide trees. There are lots of native trees such as oak, beech and hawthorn.

5 Eventually, the path bends sharply to the left leaving a much narrower, almost indistinct path to your right.

6 Follow the main path which leads downwards at a slight slope through the trees. Within a minute or so, it encounters a wider path with clearly marked edges.

7 Turning right, the path leads on through yet more woodland before emerging onto a paved estate road. **Felbrigg Hall** can be seen in the distance on the left-hand side. This is a quiet road, with only the occasional vehicle, but care still needs to be taken crossing, as vehicles can appear unexpectedly.

8 After crossing the road, walk on straight ahead. You may see some vehicles parked in small car parks on your left hand side. Ignore these and walk on into the woodland. Follow the path onwards, passing a brick wall on your right.

9 When the path suddenly joins up with a much wider path, look across it for a gateway a short distance from the path and slightly to the left. Go through the gateway. Cattle can sometimes be found grazing in this field and further onwards. Walk up the small hill towards the grove of trees at the top. Passing through the trees, walk on across the meadow to the gate at the far side. This will bring you back into the car park.

Houghton on the Hill

The 11th-century St Mary's Church in Houghton on the Hill.

A **very pretty walk, particularly in summer,** it combines walking along country lanes and field paths. There is plenty of variety in the landscape and much to keep dogs busy and active.

You can also go back in time with this walk through the countryside as it tells the story of a deserted village and the secrets that lay hidden in a ruined church!

Houghton on the Hill was a medieval village occupying the slopes overlooking the River Wissey. Now only earthworks can be seen, as the village has disappeared almost completely. The pathway past the church would once have been the main street in the village.

In the 1930s the church was abandoned and fell into ruin. In the 1990s, a group was formed to restore it – and a remarkable discovery was made. Preserved inside the 11th-century church were a series of early medieval wall paintings. These are the earliest known medieval wall paintings in Europe and are regarded as being of international importance. A pretty garden surrounds the church, creating an oasis of tranquillity and offering spectacular views across the valley. The church is regularly open to the public and visitors are welcomed.

Terrain
Country lanes and field paths. This walk can get muddy in the winter.

Where to park
Turn right in the centre of North Pickenham beside the white painted Blue Lion house. Take the first left into a quiet track lined by hedges leading up to the church. Park on the grass verge against the hedge. **OS map:** Landranger 144 Thetford and Diss (GR 864068).

How to get there
Take the A1065 south of Swaffham, and follow the signs to North Pickenham.

Nearest refreshments
There are a wide range of pubs and cafés in nearby Swaffham.

Dog factors
. . . .
Distance: 3.5 miles.
Road walking: About half the walk is via country lanes, and through the village of North Pickenham.
Livestock: Much of the area is devoted to arable farming, but horses and cattle are often found in the fields towards the end of the walk.
Stiles: One but with a dog flap.
Nearest vets: The Grove Veterinary Group, 17 Lynn St, Swaffham PE37 7AU. ☎ 01760 723739.

The Walk
. . . .

1 Walk back down the track to the road.

2 Turn left into **Houghton Lane**. Continue walking straight ahead.

Norfolk – A Dog Walker's Guide

3 At the T-junction there is a signpost for **South Pickenham**. Turn right. There are good views of the Swaffham wind turbines across the fields.

4 A short way along the road, there is a field entrance. Turn left into the field, and take the right-hand turning along the narrow tunnel-like path between tall

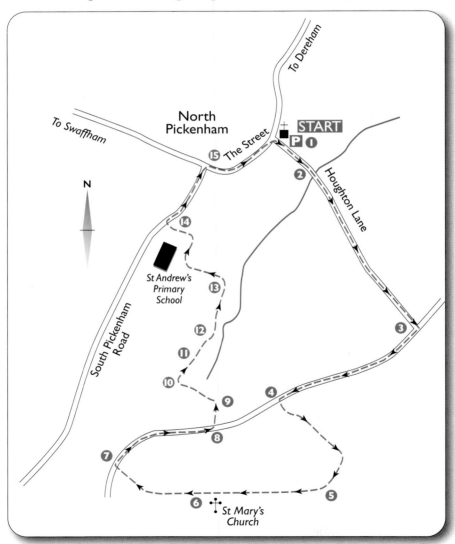

Wide spaces for your dog to run and play.

trees and hedges. The path is firm and grassy and eventually opens out into a field path along the edge of **Houghton Common**.

5 Turn right onto the wider bridleway, and walk on up the hill. It leads past the historic **church of St Mary** – which if open, is well worth a visit. Looking over the fields to the south of the church, it is hard to imagine that a village once stood here.

6 Just past the church, there is a track junction. Follow the bridleway as it winds to the right passing woodland and fields.

7 At the road, beside the historic church sign, turn right.

8 Walk down the road for a short way, looking for a left hand turning into the field. Beware – it is easy to miss this turning. The only marker is a 'Danger buried cable' sign partly hidden in the hedge. Turn left into the field entrance, and you will see a long hedge in front of you with a field to either side. Walk straight ahead towards the hedge, bearing to the left.

9 Follow the path to the left hand side of the hedge. If you look closely, you will see a hidden waymarker in the hedge – it is invisible from the roadway!

10 Continue walking beside the hedge until you reach a stile. A dog flap is available.

11 Cross the stile and walk on, following the edge of the field.

12 The path crosses a little wooden bridge over a dyke. Continue walking straight ahead.

13 Turn right at the fence and follow the edge of the field. There are sometimes horses in this field. The footpath leads past **St Andrew's Primary School** on the left. There is a dog waste bin at the end of the path.

14 At the road, turn right and follow the road to the end.

15 Turn right onto **The Street**, passing the village sign on your left. Keep walking up the road until you reach the church.

7

Fakenham Riverside

The River Wensum by Fakenham.

Walking along the river bank on the outskirts of Fakenham, it is hard to imagine that you are so close to a busy market town as well as a major racecourse. The gently rippling waters of the River Wensum are a delight at any time of the year, and there are plenty of spots where dogs can enjoy a quick dip in the river. A quick flash of bright colour may even herald the sight of a kingfisher, or a splash mark the arrival of an otter. The riverside is a haven for wildlife and has a European Special Area of Conservation status.

Norfolk – A Dog Walker's Guide

Further on is a reminder of the major role Fakenham once played in the extensive railway network which crossed Norfolk. The pretty Three Arched Bridge now stands quietly crossing the river but once it was a busy railway setting, carrying the line which linked Fakenham, Wells and Dereham. The line was closed in 1964.

At times the riverside area can be a bit muddy, and the path can narrow and become just wide enough for one person to pass. However, it makes a good, energetic walk with plenty to see no matter what the time of year.

Terrain
Riverside footpaths, sometimes uneven.

Where to park
There is a car park just off Bridge Street, near Fakenham museum. **OS map:** Landranger 132 North West Norfolk (GR 920294).

How to get there
Fakenham is a small town in north west Norfolk, just ten miles from the coast. It can be reached from the A1067 Norwich/Fakenham road, or the A148 Holt/Swaffham road, both of which bypass the town.

Nearest refreshments
The Bell in Hempton welcomes dogs (☎ 01328 864579), or try the Fakenham Garden Centre which has dog friendly tables (☎ 01328 863380).

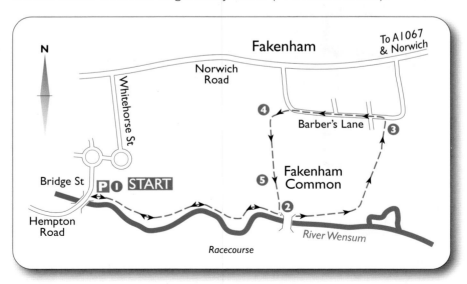

Dog factors

Distance: 3 miles.
Road walking: Virtually the entire walk can be undertaken without using streets.
Livestock: Sheep, cattle or sometimes horses may be occasionally found in the fields beyond the river.
Stiles: None.
Nearest vets: The Grove Veterinary Group, Fakenham Surgery Grove House, Holt Road, Fakenham NR21 8JG.
☎ 01328 862137.

Time for a quick dip.

Norfolk – A Dog Walker's Guide

The Walk

. . . .

1 Turn right in the car park and follow the track through a recreation area. Follow the path over the concrete bridge, then turn onto the way-marked grass path which follows the course of the river. Continue along the bank of the river for about a mile. It is a long, and sometimes muddy path. The terrain can be uneven, and there are tree roots to avoid. There are often fishermen along this stretch of the river.

2 When you reach the disused, three arched railway bridge, follow the path under it. Carry on along the river path. The path begins to wind to the left, following a small stream. Cross the stream at the wooden bridge, and follow the path uphill.

3 Follow the unmade road known as **Barber's Lane** behind the back of a row of houses.

4 At the end of the road, there is a signpost. Turn left and follow the pathway straight ahead. When you reach a minor residential road, cross over and you will see the entrance to a pathway straight ahead. The path leads down behind some houses, before passing through open fields. There are sometimes grazing animals in these fields.

5 Follow the path through the fields and back to the **Three Arched Bridge**. Then turn right and follow the river back to the car park.

The Broads, How Hill

Watching the boats on the River Ant.

An oasis of calm not far from the tourist town of Wroxham, How Hill is a wonderful place to go for a walk while gaining a glimpse into a forgotten way of life. It can be a bit disconcerting to see boats apparently moving through fields. It is only when you get closer, that the river can be seen. The watery landscape of the Broads with its rivers and marshes dominates this walk. Dogs can play in the large field near the car park. Much of the walk can be undertaken off-lead as most of the fields are used for growing crops. Dogs are not allowed onto the nature reserve itself.

How Hill is a Site of Special Scientific Interest, covering a large area of Broadland within the valley of the River Ant, just north of Ludham Bridge. Wildlife, birds and butterflies can be seen here at different times of the year.

As the path wends its way through the reed beds, there is a constant rustling as the tall reeds move in the breeze. Reeds are an important part of the environment, and the Broads Authority still cuts the reeds each year using traditional methods. The reed beds are unusual in that they are open to the rise and fall of the tidal waters. Otters have been seen in this area.

Stay on the path as the ground can be deceptive on either side – the surface can quickly turn to bog and water. You can often see motor boats and yachts as How Hill Staithe provides mooring facilities for over 30 boats.

Leaving the river behind, the route passes through fields, usually filled with arable crops. There are good views of Buttle Marsh, which contains scrapes and reedbeds designed to attract rare bitterns.

Terrain
Easy to follow bark, grass and field paths.

Where to park
There is a public car park at How Hill. **OS map:** Landranger 134 Norwich and The Broads (GR 373190).

How to get there
How Hill is signposted from the A1062 Wroxham/Potter Heigham road. The turning onto the minor roads leading to How Hill, is about half way between Ludham and Ludham Bridge.

Nearest refreshments
The Dog Inn at Ludham Bridge should welcome dogs with a name like that – and luckily it does. This friendly pub has a large beer garden and serves food ☎ 01692 630321. There is also a picnic meadow at How Hill.

Dog factors

Distance: 2 miles.
Road walking: Approximately 200 yards at the end of the walk, and crossing a very minor road part of the way round.
Livestock: None.
Stiles: None.
Nearest vets: Broadland House Veterinary Surgery, 33 High Street, Stalham NR12 9AH ☎ 01692 580171; Bridge Veterinary Practice, 63 Norwich Road, Wroxham NR12 8RX ☎ 01603 783920; Anchorage Veterinary Hospital, South Walsham Road, Acle NR13 3EA ☎ 01493 750255.

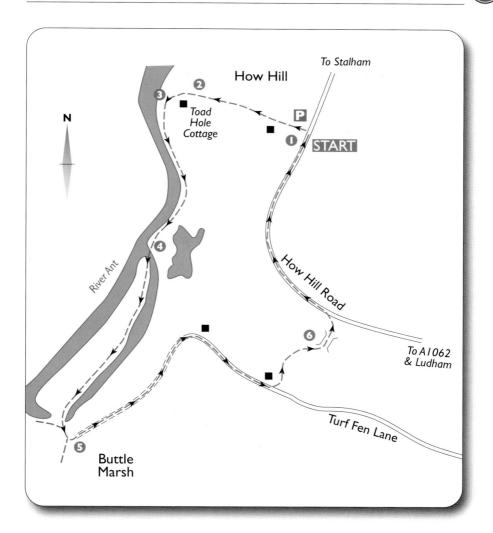

The Walk

. . . .

1 Walk across the picnic meadow towards the hedge. Go through the gate and down to **Toad Hole Cottage**.

2 Follow the path straight ahead past the cottage and down to the river.

Ready to explore the broad.

3 Turn left at the river. This is initially a wide path with a hard surface running alongside the river bank. Within a short time, the path narrows and becomes grassy. Walking through tall banks of reeds and open fields, boats can frequently be seen passing on the river.

4 Look for a gate on the left-hand side of the path. Go through the gate and follow the field path away from the river. Keep the dyke on your right hand side, and walk up towards the trees at the far end of the field. There are wonderful views of the lakes on the **Buttle Marshes**. Water birds may also be seen. At the top of the field, ignore the path turning to the left. Walk ahead until you reach **Turf Fen Lane**.

5 Cross over the lane to continue walking along the footpath on the other side. This is a very pretty path especially in spring time when snowdrops and catkins are in bloom. Having passed the houses on the left hand side, the path becomes a field path again. This section of the path is narrower, and can be a bit rough underfoot and muddy.

6 Cross over the small bridge and walk on through the area of tall rushes. Follow the path through a gap in the hedge. This brings you out onto a tarmac road. Turn left and follow the road back to **How Hill car park**.

River Wensum at Swanton Morley

A field path by the River Wensum.

I t is hard to believe that the bustling market town of Dereham and a major army barracks are only a short distance away from this tranquil countryside. Walking peacefully along, it is easy to feel isolated and away from everyday life. Along the way there are lots of opportunities for dogs to play, swim and paddle in the river and beck, and if there is no livestock in the fields, dogs can be let off the leash for a good run. It makes a perfect walk for lively dogs like Freddie, Melodie and Scamp!

The Wensum River is one of the prettiest in Norfolk. It has been designated a special area of conservation and is one of the UK's most important chalk rivers. This stretch of the river passes through the Carrick Estate and is definitely one of the best areas to see all kinds of wildlife. Swans, mallards, Canadian geese, pheasants and tufted ducks are all frequent visitors – and keen eyes may even see the flash of a kingfisher darting above the water. During the summer there are lots of small white butterflies.

The paths can get muddy, so strong footwear is essential. There are also several gates to be opened on this walk, always make sure that they are closed afterwards. All are nice and wide - easy to open.

Swanton Morley is a small village with a history dating back to the Domesday Book. There are military links too – the village used to be home to an important RAF station which has since been taken over by the Army. It can be disconcerting seeing road signs warning of tanks crossing – this refers to the nearby Robertson Barracks where a tank regiment is based. There are also American links – the Angel pub in the village has ancestral links to President Abraham Lincoln.

Terrain
Fields, riverside, tracks and tarmac road. A mostly level surface but can be muddy.

Where to park
There is a car park at Hunter's Hall. **OS map:** Landranger 133 (GR 029166 / NR20 4JT).

How to get there
From the A47, take the B1147 to Swanton Morley. Drive through the village, and turn right at Darby's Free House. The pub is set a little back from the road, and is on a bend. This is Elsing Road. Take the third turning on the right, marked Hunter's Hall. This is a long drive leading up to the car park.

Nearest refreshments
The friendly Darby's Free House has a large beer garden with a children's play area and a large and varied menu ☎ 01362 637647.

Dog factors
. . . .

Distance: 3 miles.
Road walking: One minor road has to be crossed, and returning involves a short walk of about half a mile along a quiet road. There are no pavements.
Livestock: Cattle and sheep may be found in the fields. They are rotated around the site and many fields may be empty for long periods.
Stiles: None.
Off lead: Yes.
Nearest vets: The Grove, 1 Newton Court, Norwich Road, East Dereham NR20 3ES. ☎ 01362 696772.

The Walk

1 Walk down the drive and cross the road. Follow the path towards **Castle Farm**.

2 Before reaching the farm buildings, look for a large gap in the hedge on the right-hand side. This leads into a field. Take this turning and walk straight across the centre of the field.

3 At the far edge of the field, turn left following the line of the hedge. Beware of rabbit holes, if you have a dog who finds it fun to investigate them!

4 Go through the gate. Cross a farm track and walk straight ahead, across the field.

5 Cross a dyke via the turf-covered bridge and continue walking ahead up the river bank.

6 Turn right and follow the path along the **River Wensum**. The path follows a raised bank edged with reeds above the river, but there are lower sections in

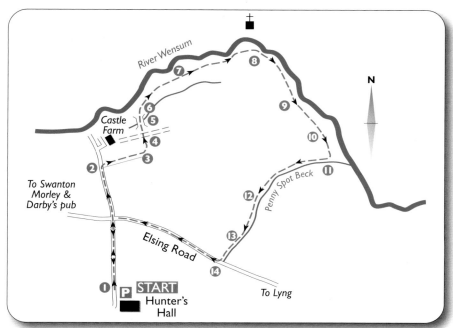

places where dogs can gain access to the river. Take care passing the reed beds as dogs can mistake these boggy areas for solid ground.

There is a field on the right hand side. If there is no livestock in the field, then dogs can be let off the leash.

7 Go through the gate at the end of the path and follow the path away from the river. This section can get a bit rough underfoot.

8 Go through the gate, and continue walking ahead.

9 At the seat, turn right. The path goes round a small pool marking the end of the drainage ditch. Swans sometimes swim here.

10 Turn left, and walk straight up the field towards the gate.

11 Go through the gate. At this point, the path follows **Penny Spot Beck**, a stretch of water filled dyke. This is quite wide and moderately deep, with fewer reed beds. There are several low lying areas where dogs can swim, paddle and play in the water.

12 Moving away from the dyke, the path follows the left hand side of the field. It can get very muddy and boggy. Strong footwear is essential. Starting as a grass path, it eventually becomes a farm track with rubble underfoot.

13 Go through the gate and carry on walking down the path towards the road.

14 Turn right into **Elsing Road**. This is a quiet road, used mainly by farm traffic and some cars. Walk along the road, until you reach the driveway to **Hunter's Hall**. Turn left, and follow the drive back to the car park.

Time for a quick river dip.

Ringland Hills

A bright day on the Ringland Hills.

Ringland is one of the prettiest villages in Norfolk. Occupying a valley site between the Ringland Hills and the Wensum river, it is very popular during the summer with visitors enjoying the riverside setting. Swans and wild ducks often feed beside the river, and the shallow water by the Swan Inn is perfect for dogs to splash and play in.

This is another of Freddie, Melodie and Scamp's favourite walks. The combination of fields, woodland, hills and water make for a perfect stroll at any time of the year. Although one of the shorter walks, the varying gradients and terrain can make walking quite challenging at times. It is possible to let dogs off leads in places, but watch out for the possibility of livestock down by the river.

It is a very relaxing stroll as there is so much to see. There is wildlife in the fields and by the river, while reminders of the past are always present. Parson Woodforde, the 18th-century author of *The Diary of a Country Parson* was rector at the church of St Peter from 1776 to 1803. The renowned painter, Sir Alfred Munning, described the area as, 'One of our loveliest districts of all in this pleasant country,' using it as the setting for his painting, *Ponies on Ringland Hills*. During the Second World War, the valley had an important defensive role and concrete tank traps still remain along the river banks.

Terrain
Varied gradients and a hill, field tracks and country lanes.

Where to park
There are parking spots beside the river in Ringland opposite the Swan Inn. **OS map:** Landranger 133 North East Norfolk (GR 141137).

How to get there
At the roundabout at the western end of the A47 Norwich bypass, take the turning towards Ringland. At the next road junction, turn left and drive straight on until you reach the village. These are very narrow roads and steep in places, but there are passing places available.

Nearest refreshments
The Swan Inn is opposite the village green in Ringland and overlooks the River Wensum. This lovely pub welcomes children and dogs. ☎ 01603 868214.

Dog factors
. . . .

Distance: 2.5 miles.
Road walking: About a quarter of the walk is along minor village roads, generally without pavements. The wide trackway leading up to Royal Hill is sometimes used by farm vehicles.
Livestock: Sheep and cattle may be present in the fields near the river.
Stiles: 1.
Nearest vets: Taverham Veterinary Surgery Fir Covert Road, Taverham NR8 6HT. ☎ 01603 867330.

The Walk
. . . .

1 Cross over the road and walk straight ahead down **The Street**. The route takes you past the village green with its picturesque sign. On the way, look for the house with the monkeys in the garden! Keep walking ahead until you reach the **church of St Peter**.

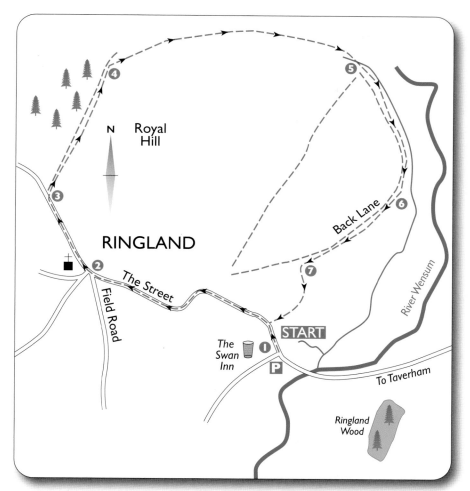

② Turn right, walking past the **Village Hall** which will be on your left hand side. Originally, this was known as the Reading Room and was also a Methodist chapel.

③ Passing the end of a row of houses, look for a turning to the right. This is a wide sandy track going uphill. It is quite steep. The fields on either side are used for growing crops. At the top of **Royal Hill**, enjoy the spectacular views across the village and the Wensum valley. Continue down the track towards the valley bottom.

Norfolk – A Dog Walker's Guide

4 Passing a house on the left, the hedgelined path becomes much greener and grassy. Cross the stile. This is an unusual one. Instead of climbing over, you have to pull the sides apart and walk through it. Doing this one-handed is not always easy, especially if you have a large dog trying to go through so take care. Turn right, and follow the grassy path beside the hedgerow.

5 Go through the next stile and follow the track onwards, veering left towards some poplar trees. The path begins to get narrower and at times wet and a bit muddy as it passes through a low lying marshy meadow. The river can be seen in the distance.

6 Ignore the little bridge passing over a slow moving, but deep stream and continue to walk straight ahead. Eventually, the path emerges beside a house and a lamp post. Turn right and walk on down **Back Lane**.

7 A few minutes' walk leads you to a turning to the left signposted with a footpath marker. Take this turning and walk on. A narrow, grassy pathway, it will bring you back to the main street. Turn left to return to the **Swan Inn**.

The village green at Ringland.

Whitlingham Wood

*The statue of a boy wearing goggles and a snorkel
is carved from a tree stump.*

Broads, river and woodland all combine to create an extremely unusual walk. Where else can you cover over 10,000 years of history in just two miles?

Norfolk – A Dog Walker's Guide

Whitlingham Woods have a long history. Prehistoric people keen to obtain supplies of flint extensively quarried the area, leaving behind deep wooded quarries. In Victorian times, more quarrying took place to fuel a constantly burning kiln creating lime that was ferried down to Norwich and Great Yarmouth via the adjacent river Yare.

Well trained dogs can happily explore off leash but it is best to keep them in sight, as there is a major road at the one side of the woods; and deep Neolithic quarries on the other side. This still provides plenty of room for them to explore the intriguing scents and smells of a woodland.

On the southern edge of the wood, gravel removal in the 20th century led to the building of the A47 bypass around Norwich, as well as local shopping centres and a hospital. The resultant quarry was turned into a lake known as Whitlingham Great Broad which now provides extensive leisure facilities and a wildlife reserve.

The area is extremely attractive at all times of the year. Fishermen, boats and cruisers use the deep, fast flowing river. Wild geese and other birds nest along the river and Broad. A mix of deciduous and evergreen trees can be found throughout the woodland. The views through the quarries are quite spectacular – especially when you are at the very top and realise that you cannot see the bottom!

Terrain
Steep gradients in places, steps and bark paths.

Where to park
The road narrows after passing the Country Park car park. There are numerous speed bumps so it is important to drive slowly. There are passing places. Shortly after passing a white house on your right-hand side, you will come to a car park on the right. There is a small charge for parking. **OS map:** Landranger 134 Norwich and the Broads (GR 269078).

Dog factors

. . . .

Distance: 2 miles (or 3 miles for the longer route).
Road walking: Small amount along a quiet side road at the end of the walk, and crossing the same road.
Livestock: None.
Stiles; None.
Nearest vets: Willow Veterinary Clinic, 202 Thorpe Road, Norwich NR1 1TJ. ☎ 01603 300814.

How to get there

Whitlingham is on the eastern outskirts of Norwich. Leave the A47 at the Norwich/Trowse exit and drive towards Norwich until you reach a T junction. Turn right, and keep in the right-hand lane. Turn right at the next roundabout. Follow the road straight ahead until you reach a turning marked Whitlingham Country Park & no access to Kirby Bedon. Take this turning, and drive straight ahead past the entrance to the Country Park.

Nearest refreshments

There is a café at the Whitlingham Country Park centre ☎ 01603 756094 or try the Barn Café ☎ 07407 709537. There is also space for riverside and meadow picnics close to the car park at the entrance to the woods.

The Walk

· ·

1 Cross the road and turn right, walking alongside the river bank for about five minutes, passing a wooden statue of a boy.

2 When the path opens out into a grassy glade, turn right. Go across the road, and through the gate.

3 Follow the path straight ahead through the woodland. It is a hard path, well maintained and a bit stony.

4 The path leads to a glade containing the remains of a limestone kiln together with interpretation boards explaining how it worked. Daubenton's, Natterer's and brown long-eared bats now occupy the disused kiln. The glade is quite shady and very atmospheric.

5 Turn right and take the path up a long flight of steps. There is a hand rail. Alternatively, if you prefer an easier gradient, retrace your steps out of the clearing and you will find a gentler path leading upwards on the left-hand side.

6 Whichever path you take, when you reach the top follow the path straight ahead. It will eventually reach a T junction with another path. Turn left and then walk straight on along the path.

7 The wide bark path leads upwards and through woodland. Well maintained, the paths are accessible at all times of the year. There are lots of blackberries in this area during the autumn, and the leaf colour can be fantastic.

Norfolk – A Dog Walker's Guide

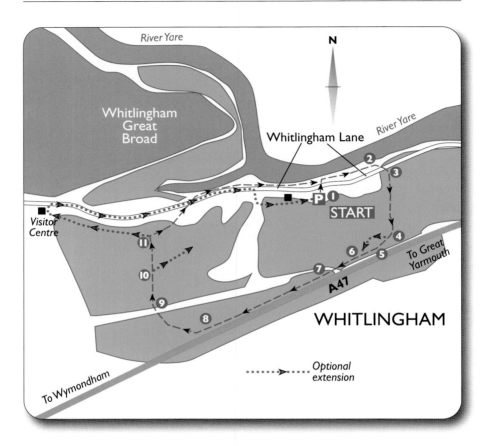

8 The path leads along the top of **Whitlingham Woods**, adjacent to the **A47**. This is a very busy, major road and although the traffic cannot be seen, it can be heard.

On the other side of the path are more trees and the steep walls of the Neolithic flint quarries. The quarries are very deep and filled with trees and undergrowth. Some of the quarries are railed so that you can go near the edge and look down. There are several small paths on the right-hand side which lead to the edge of one of the quarries, and eventually return to join the main path.

9 Follow the wide main path onwards. The tree cover becomes thicker as the path moves away from the quarries, before heading southwards and offering more views across the deep wooded sides of another quarry.

10 The path eventually reaches a T junction. You can choose between turning right for a gentle gradient down to the car park, or turning left down a very steep flight of steps.

11 At the bottom of the steps is another T junction. Turn right for a gentle stroll through woodland and meadow to the road. Then turn right, walking along the road for a few minutes before reaching another right-hand turning into the woodland. Take this turning, then turn left to follow the path back to the car park.

*Alternatively, at the bottom of the steep steps you can opt for a longer walk. Turn left and follow the path across the meadow to the **Whitlingham Country Visitor Centre**. Walk back along the side of **Whitlingham Great Broad** until you reach a path leading to the right. Take this turning, then turn left and follow the footpath along the road to reach the car park.*

A beautiful day at Whitlingham Great Broad.

Burgh Castle

Wide open spaces to explore.

On this stimulating walk you can explore the past and enjoy some spectacular views, while giving your dog a walk that it will thoroughly enjoy. There is plenty of room to have a run and play, while also discovering a vast range of enticing smells and environments from riverside, fields and castle.

Burgh Castle is an impressive place. Now in the care of English Heritage, it is one of the few remaining Roman forts in the east of England. Three sides of the fort known as *Gariannonum* survive. Originally, these walls would have been 57 metres high; now they are around 45 metres high and vary from between 2.2 and 3.3 metres wide. There are large, drum-shaped bastions at each corner facing outwards – attacking this fort would not have been easy! One side of the fort has a gap in the wall and a mound inside. This dates back to when the Normans altered the fort, adding a motte and knocking down part of the wall to make a smaller fortified space. Dogs have to be on a lead at the castle and it is free to visit.

Early morning Sunday visitors may encounter a surprise. The sound of clashing swords and shouts from a group of people dressed in jerkins, helmets and cloaks can often be heard as a group of local Anglo-Saxon re-enactors practise their fighting techniques at the site.

The views from the castle are truly spectacular. The marshes and Breydon Water stretch for miles into the distance, and you can often spot leisure boats on the river.

Terrain
Firm field and riverside paths. Beware the potential boggy areas among the reeds as these can be very muddy.

Where to park
A free car park at Burgh Castle. **OS map:** Landranger 134 Norwich and The Broads (GR 480051).

How to get there
Burgh Castle is 3 miles west of Great Yarmouth, at the southern end of Breydon Water. Take the A12 from Great Yarmouth, then the A143 at Gorleston. Follow signs for minor roads to Bradwell, then Burgh Castle.

Nearest refreshments
Queens Head, Burgh Castle (NR31 9QQ) allows dogs inside but also has a beer garden. It serves food from Friday to Sunday ☎ 01493 780363.

Dog factors
Distance: 3 miles.
Road walking: None.
Livestock: None.
Stiles: None.
Nearest vets The Veterinary Hospital, Magdalen Way, Gorleston, Great Yarmouth NR31 7BN. ☎ 01493 661833.
Pets At Home, Unit 4 , Pasteur Road, Thamesfield Way, Great Yarmouth NR31 0DH. ☎ 01493 442487

The Walk

• •

1 Leave the car park by the kissing gate and turn right towards the church tower in the distance.

2 At the information point, turn right and walk down the path past the church to the gate.

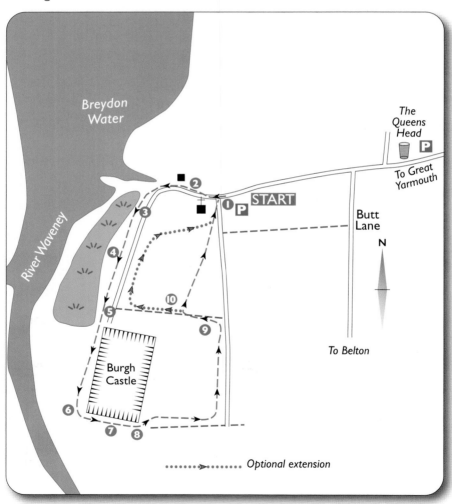

3 Turn left and walk on for about a minute.

4 A footpath leading to the left can be seen marked by a signpost. Take this turning. There is a dog waste bin near the signpost.

5 The path is quite a long one, passing initially through trees, then beside a reed bed. The terrain is firm, but can get muddy in the autumn and winter. There are good views across the marshes towards the windmills in the distance and boats on the river. The reeds can prove irresistible for dogs – but beware. It is boggy and wet!

6 At the end of the path, there is an option to turn right and stroll down to the river bank where there is a small quay. Alternatively, turn left up the steps to enter **Burgh Castle** and explore the massive structure that remains. There is a wide open space inside the walls. In places it is possible to climb up onto the walls for some extremely good views across the marshes and surrounding countryside.

7 Leaving the fort by the path leading down to the little quay, walk up the path and take the first turning to the right.

8 This leads into a massive field. Walk straight ahead following the hedge line. During the summer this is a wild flower meadow. At the end of the field turn left, and then left again at the far edge.

9 The path leads to a gap in the hedge where there is a junction of three paths. Walk straight ahead following the hedge line. This field lies to the outside of Burgh Castle and would have been where a small **Roman town** serving the fort existed.

10 At the next gap, there is a choice. Turn right, cross the small lane and go diagonally across the next field which leads back to the car park.

Alternatively, turn left and follow the line of the hedge almost to the bottom of the field. There is a turning to the right, which takes you diagonally across the next field. Follow the small path to the right, to gain more views of the river and marshes. There is a seat here for anyone who wants to take a short break.

At the end of the path, turn left and walk diagonally across the field, heading for the gap in the hedge. Walk down the next field to the field entrance and turn right. This path leads back to the car park.

The imposing stone walls of Burgh Castle.

Denver Mill

Denver windmill stands proudly against the skyline.

ogs can be let off the leash for a good part of this walk. The secluded path bordering fields is great for dogs to safely explore as there are hedges and fencing where there is livestock. Exploring the area around Denver Mill provides some wonderful views across open countryside. This is a peaceful walk through open fields, along a secluded tunnel-like path edged with tall trees and hedges and finishing in the streets of Denver village.

The wide fenland skies seem to go on forever in this low lying landscape. Denver is at the heart of the Fens – an area which was purely marshland and flood plain for many centuries. In 1651, Cornelius Vermuyden built the first sluice designed to drain the Fens, control the rivers and create land for agriculture. The site was chosen because it is at the junction of five rivers. Since then the sluice has been upgraded several times. Denver is still the focal point of the defence system which protects the Fens from flooding by sea and river.

Over the centuries, much of the peat-based farmland has dried out and contracted. The result is a landscape bisected by ditches, rivers and drains where often the fields are lower than the adjacent watercourses.

Denver Windmill was one of the last remaining working windmills in Norfolk. The existing building was constructed in 1835, replacing an earlier post mill. It appeared in an episode of the TV series, 'Allo 'Allo entitled *Fighting with Windmills*. Until 2011, it had four great sails. There was an accident when one of the giant sails broke. Debris was thrown throughout the site and at the time there was a visiting school party. Luckily, no one was hurt and funds are being raised to repair and reinstall the sails. A Grade II listed building, it was in the care of the Norfolk Historic Buildings Trust from 1995 to 2016, when it was purchased by Two Rivers Brewery in Denver. The windmill still works and guided tours are available. It is open all year for visitors (☎ 01366 389701).

Terrain
A mix of pavements, field tracks and grass paths.

Where to park
Free of charge at Denver Windmill.

How to get there
Denver is signed from the A10, just south of Downham Market. **OS map:** Landranger 143 Ely and Wisbech (GR 605012).

Nearest refreshments
The Blackstone Engine Bar or the tearooms at Denver Windmill (☎ 01366 389701) or the Bell Inn, Ely Road, Denver (☎ 01366 381127 / PE38 0DW). The Bell serves food every day except Mondays. Dogs are allowed in the beer garden.

Dog factors
Distance: 2.2 miles (3.2 for the longer route).
Road walking: About a third of the walk uses minor roads round the village, mostly with a pavement.
Livestock: Sheep and cattle sometimes graze in the fields.
Stiles: None.
Nearest vets: The Crossings Veterinary Centre, St. John's Way, Downham Market PE38 0QQ. ☎ 01366 382219.

The Walk

. . . .

❶ Leaving the car park, return to the road and turn left past a big willow tree. Walk about 150 yards down the road. This will bring you to a gate on your left marked '**Norfolk Walks**'.

❷ Go through the gate, and walk straight ahead across the field. This is rough meadowland attracting a wide range of wildlife including green woodpeckers. Cattle can sometimes be found grazing in the field. There is a grassy dyke on the left-hand side.

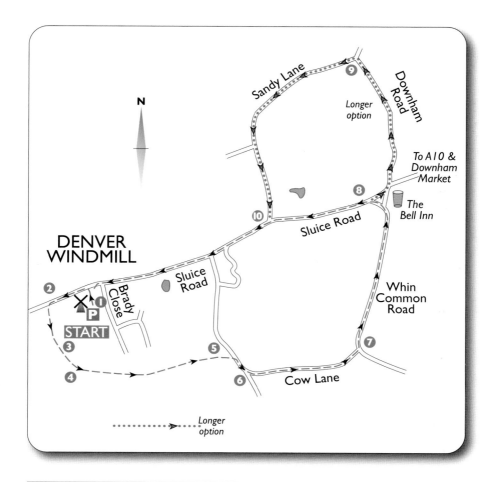

3 Just past a great, up rooted tree trunk there is a grassy path leading to the left. Follow this path down a hollow and over to a gate. Passing through the gate, there is a short boardwalk across muddy ground. The path wends its way slightly to the right.

4 A short way further on, the path leads into a long, sheltered, tunnel like route between tall hedges and trees which almost curves over at the top. Gaps in the hedges give glimpses across fields on both sides, as well as views into the village. The path is quite good all year round offering firm walking on grass, earth and leaves.

5 150 yards further on, the path opens out to a T junction with a wide farm track. Turn left, and walk along the track following the line of the hedge. There are open fields on the other side of the track.

6 After walking about 130 yards, turn left into **Cow Lane**. After a short while, you will begin to see houses appearing on the right-hand side.

7 This track turns left into a broad road with no pavements. This is **Whin Common Road**. Walk down the road until you reach a T junction. An old fashioned water pump can be seen on the right-hand side. Turn left and walk down **Sluice Road** until you reach the windmill.

8 A longer walk is possible if you turn right at the T junction of **Whin Common Road** and **Sluice Road**. Follow the road to the left up through the village past the war memorial. This road is slightly uphill.

9 Just before reaching the main road, turn sharply left and follow the path over to the gateway leading to **Sandy Lane**. Walk down **Sandy Lane**. This is a long, broad track with no footpaths. It leads through fields and past some houses.

10 At the T-junction with **Sluice Road**, turn right and walk back to **Denver Windmill** which can be seen in the distance.

14

Stoke Ferry

The River Wessey flows through Stoke Ferry.

Here you can enjoy rivers, fields and a village in this gentle walk at the edge of the Fenland countryside. Stoke Ferry is an attractive village approximately midway between Downham Market and Thetford. Although dogs are best kept on leash while walking on the road, off leash along the river and through the fields is possible at most times of the year. The river itself is not accessible as fencing prevents access.

The Fens were originally a marshy, wetland area. From the 17th century onwards, much of the Fens were drained to provide fertile agricultural land.

It has resulted in the creation of the typical low lying, flat landscape which seems to stretch for miles without any breaks.

This is a relaxing circular walk, which offers the opportunity to explore several facets of the area. The rich soil is perfect for agriculture and closer to the river animals are grazed all year round. Passing through Stoke Ferry, the River Wissey is a quiet, tranquil river providing a home to wildlife and birds as well as several houseboats. The open fenland landscape gives you superb vistas across the surrounding area.

Stoke Ferry itself is a typical fenland village with many old stone houses. Hints of their past life as shops can be seen if you look carefully; for example, The Old Chemist's Shop still has its deep display window even though it has now been turned into a house.

All Saints Church is a distinctive building with an unusual bell tower. The 15th-century building no longer holds services, but is used by the local community for exhibitions, concerts and other functions.

Terrain
Pavements, unpaved roads, field tracks and bridleways.

Where to park
Free of charge at the Blue Bell Inn, Lynn Road. **OS map:** Landranger 143 Ely and Wisbech (GR 702003).

How to get there
Stoke Ferry is 6.5 miles south east of Downham Market going towards Thetford. It is just off the A134. Take the turning into Stoke Ferry signposted from the roundabout at the junction with the B1112. Drive through the village until you see the Blue Bell Inn on your right.

Dog factors
Distance: 2.2 miles.
Road walking: Less than a third of the walk is via village roads, most of which have pavements.
Livestock: Sheep, horses and cattle may be found in fields near the river. Other parts of the walk pass through fields devoted to crop farming.
Stiles: 1.
Nearest vets: The Hollies Vets, Paradise Road, Downham Market PE38 9JE. ☎ 01366 386655; The Crossings Veterinary Centre St. John's Way, Downham Market PE38 0QQ. ☎ 01366 382219.

Nearest refreshments

The Blue Bell Inn is an excellent pub filled with character and serves food every day except Mondays. Dogs are welcome in the garden and outside the inn, but should not be brought inside. ☎ 01366 502056 / PE33 9SW.

The Walk

1 Leaving the car park, turn left and follow the **Lynn Road** through the village.

2 When the road divides, keep to the left and walk down the **High Street**, past **All Saints Church** with its unusual bell tower. The **High Street** leads into **Bridge Road**.

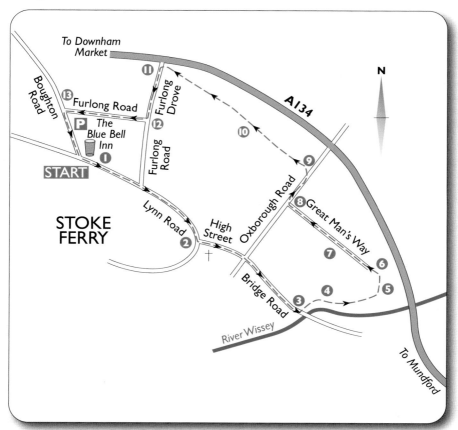

3 Just before the bridge, look for a bridleway on the left hand side of the road. There is a signpost marking the location. Turn left down the grassy path. Go through the gate at the end and continue walking straight ahead.

4 This part of the walk is quite a long one, following the course of the **River Wissey**. The path is set back from the river bank. There is no direct river access due to fences on the right-hand side but there are good views across the river. Several houseboats are moored along here.

Follow the path straight ahead, through a series of gates which need to be fastened each time. There are fields on the left-hand side which sometimes provide grazing for sheep.

The grassy path can get a little rough and overgrown during the summer but is generally well maintained.

5 At the end of the path, go through the gate and turn left. Follow the path down to the next gate.

6 Go through the gate, which is almost directly ahead of you and walk down the wide grassy path. There are houses on the right hand side and a hedge on the left.

7 The walk continues through the next gate which leads onto an unpaved road known as **Great Man's Way**. A long straight track, it passes numerous houses mainly on the right-hand side and open fields offering pleasant views across the countryside.

8 At the T junction, turn right into **Oxborough Road**. This is a minor road leading out of the village. There are pavements.

9 Walk along **Oxborough Road** for about 180 yards and turn left onto a wide unpaved path at the end of the row of houses. This path merges into a grassy track leading into an open field.

10 At the end of the grassy track, there is a rough field path which goes almost diagonally across the field, towards the main **A134** road which can be seen on the right-hand side.

11 At the far end of the field, almost at the junction with the **A134**, there is a stile. After crossing the stile, turn left down **Furlong Drove**. This is a public road with pavements.

12 Take the first right-hand turning after the churchyard into **Furlong Road**. This is a quiet, narrow, tree-lined, residential road with very little traffic. There are no pavements so walk carefully. At the end of the road, you will reach a T-junction.

13 Turn left down **Boughton Road**. A few minutes further on, you will reach another road junction. Turn left into **Lynn Road**, and you will see the **Blue Bell Inn** directly ahead.

The flat landscape of the fens.

Oxborough Village Walk

The great tower and spire of St John, Oxborough, fell down in 1948.

Oxburgh or Oxborough? Confusion can easily reign when you search for this village on the map as it is spelt differently from the better-known National Trust property located in the village.

Oxburgh Hall is a beautiful, moated 15th-century manor house built in 1482 by Sir Edmund Bedingfeld. On display in the Hall are a series of spectacular embroideries made by Mary, Queen of Scots and her ladies between 1569 and 1585. The gatehouse has a hidden priest's hole, while out in the woods is a small chapel. Although the Hall is now in the care of the National Trust, it remains a family home for members of the Bedingfeld family. The gardens contain an elaborate parterre as well as an orchard filled with traditional varieties of apples and pears. See the National Trust website for visiting times.

Oxborough itself is a tranquil village set amid a landscape of mainly arable fields, although there is also some livestock farming. Much of the walk follows quiet country roads; mainly used by farm vehicles and the occasional car. Walking across the fields, the wide landscape gives a feeling of openness, as though you are far from everything. Dogs can be let off leads especially when crossing fields as long as there is no livestock present. But beware – during the summer time, small dogs can easily get lost among the tall growing crops!

The variety of road verges, hedges and fields present lots of interesting smells for curious dogs. It combines to make for a very pleasant, relaxing walk through attractive scenery. Much of the farmland is protected as it is a Site of Special Scientific Interest and at dusk you can glimpse bats and owls in the sky.

Terrain
A mix of quiet minor roads and field paths.

Where to park
At the pub if you are using it for refreshments, alternatively around the village green or at Oxburgh Hall if it is open. **OS map:** Landranger 143 Ely and Wisbech (GR 743014).

How to get there
Follow the National Trust signs from the A134 Downham Market/Thetford Road. A minor road leads to the village of Oxborough.

Nearest refreshments
The beautiful Bedingfeld Arms serves food and allows dogs in the bar area, there is also a beer garden. ☎ 01366 328300 / PE33 9PS.

Dog factors

Distance: 3.2 miles.
Road walking: The majority of this walk is along minor roads without pavements.
Livestock: Free-range pigs may be found in some of the fields edging the roads.
Stiles: 2.
Nearest vets: The Hollies Vets, Paradise Road, Downham Market PE38 9JE. ☎ 01366 386655; The Grove Veterinary Group, 17 Lynn Street, Swaffham. ☎ 01760 723739.

The Walk

1 Keeping the church behind you, walk across the village green. Cross over the road into **Eastmoor Road**. Walk straight ahead down the road. It quickly changes into a quiet, green lane edged by fields.

Norfolk – A Dog Walker's Guide

2 Look for a fingerpost on the left-hand side of the road, marking a footpath. Turn right and walk across the field. The path is on a slight diagonal heading towards a bank of trees on the far side. It can get a bit wet and muddy. Climb up and over the bank into the next field. Walk straight on, along another slightly diagonal path heading for the corner. This leads onto a grassy field track.

3 Turn left at the field track. This is quite a wide, firm track lined by hedges on the right and trees, especially birch on the left.

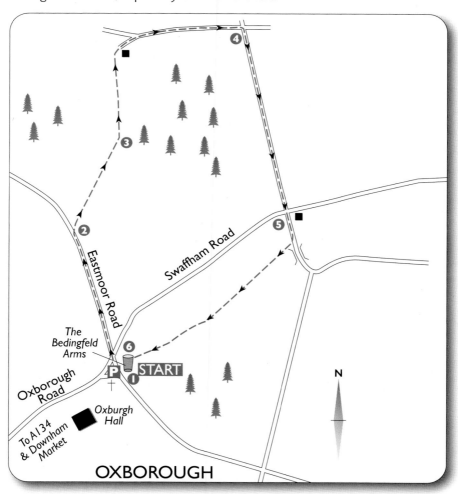

4 At the road junction, turn right and walk down the road. It leads between fields used for growing crops and also livestock farming. Edged by grass verges and hedges, this is a very quiet minor road used only by occasional cars or farm vehicles. At the crossroads marked by a fingerpost, walk straight ahead.

5 Go past a house on the left. Soon afterwards, there is a 30 mph traffic sign and a bridge. Just before reaching the bridge, turn right at the stile. After crossing the stile, walk straight ahead keeping to the left edge of the field. Dogs can be let off the leash if there is no livestock in the field. Although the side of the field widens out, keep walking ahead aiming for the big tree and hedgerow in the distance. Go past the tree and keep to the left of the hedge. At the top of the field, go over the stile and into the next field. Walk ahead, and follow the path down the field. The hedge will now be on your left.

6 The path comes out a circular clearing. Cross the road, and walk ahead keeping the hedge on your right. Just before a farmhouse, there is a stile on the right through the hedge. Cross the stile, then turn right and follow the path down past the telephone box. This path eventually widens out into a road, which leads back to Oxborough and the **Bedingfeld Arms**.

Following a grassy trail.

Old Buckenham

Walking under a wide open sky.

Dogs will enjoy the variety of landscapes, as well as the opportunity to play on the common where they can be let off the leash. Most exciting of all for any dog is the pretty walk through the woodland and fields with its enticing smells.

Old Buckenham is believed to have the largest village green in Britain covering around 40 acres of green space as well as numerous duck ponds. A sprawling village, it has many pretty thatched houses and a medieval church with an unusual octagonal tower. It makes for a very peaceful, relaxing walk suitable for all weathers and seasons.

The village dates back to the Norman invasion when William d'Albini was granted land in the area. Although the site developed as a village, d'Albini decided it was not suitable for his castle. A better location was chosen about a mile away in what became known as New Buckenham. It was here that a small market developed close to the castle.

Strolling around the quiet country lanes, common land and woodland that make up this walk, there are plenty of opportunities to discover the history of the area. Along the way, there is a windmill dating back to 1818 which has a tower with the largest diameter in England; while further on there is the Askew Agricultural Museum based on the agricultural heritage of the area.

The incessant cawing of rooks enlivened the stroll along the woodland path, although it is essential to watch your step when nearing the little pool as it is all too easy to trip over the earth mound. It offered a quick opportunity for the dogs to enjoy a drink and a paddle. An inquisitive pair of Shire horses greeted us as we emerged near their field – only to find them cantering across the field to greet us again at the far side.

Terrain

Country lanes, fields and woodland path.

Where to park

On the Green near the children's play area or at the Ox and Plough. **OS map:** Landranger 144 Thetford and Diss. (GR 065914 / NR17 1RN).

How to get there

Old Buckenham is just off the B1077 which joins the B1113 at New Buckenham.

Nearest refreshments

The Ox and Plough on the Green in Old Buckenham is a friendly pub and serves food every day except Wednesdays. It provided a welcome break at the end of the walk and is very dog friendly. In the summer, tables out on the common offer a good opportunity to sit back and relax with a drink (☎ 01953 860970 / NR17 1RN).

Dog factors

Distance: 4 miles.
Road walking: About three quarters of the walk uses minor roads and village roads without footpaths.
Livestock: Cattle and sheep may be found in some of the fields adjoining the roads, and horses in the field at the end of the woodland section.
Stiles: None.
Nearest vets: Connaught Veterinary Surgery, Station Road, Attleborough NR17 2AS. ☎ 01953 454945; The Old Golf House Veterinary Group, Daglas House, Connaught Plain, Attleborough NR17 2EJ. ☎ 01953 451100.

Norfolk – A Dog Walker's Guide

The Walk

. . . .

1 Turn right out of the pub car park and walk past the village hall.

2 Turn right onto the common. Follow the road past the pollarded tree up to the signpost. Cross over the **Attleborough** road, and walk straight ahead.

At the next crossroads, turn right and walk on past the **Green**.

3

Turn left down a quiet lane which leads past a windmill and out of the village.

4 Continue walking ahead through the peaceful countryside of fields and hedges full of mixed varieties of ivy, hawthorn, oak and beech.

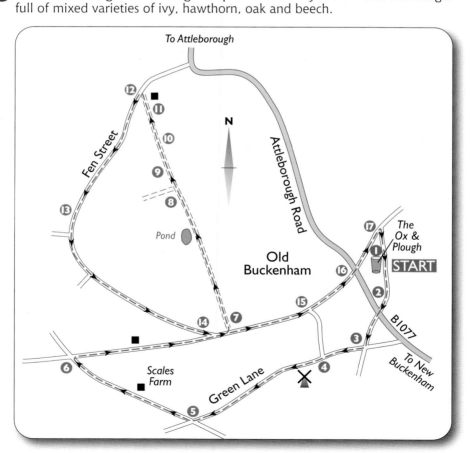

5 A Give Way sign marks the next crossroads. Turn right down **Grove Road**, past the signpost marked **New Buckenham/Hargham**. You will be walking in the direction of **Hargham**. The way leads past **Askew Agricultural Museum** at **Scales Farm**. The road is quite narrow but there are passing places.

6 At the junction marked **Shropham/Old Buckenham**, turn right into **Old Buckenham Road**. The route leads past a turkey farm and into the edge of Old Buckenham.

7 Just after passing the 30mph sign, there is a sign for a public footpath on the left hand side of the road. There is a dog refuse bin at the entrance. Turn left up the footpath. This is a very pleasant grass path which is quite wide at this

Old Buckenham windmill.

point. Surrounded by tall hedges and trees, there are constant glimpses into neighbouring fields. Ignore any gaps in the hedges – there is no public access allowed into these fields.

Half way along the path there is a small natural pond on the left. There is quite a steep drop down to the pond. The spot is marked by a large mound of earth in the middle of the path, and lots of tree roots. The path begins to get narrower.

8 When the path bends sharply to the left, look for the entrance to the field on your right. Turn right into the field. A signpost marks the spot.

9 Having entered the field, turn left and walk straight ahead following the line of the hedge. There is also a deep ditch.

10 At the end of the field, go through the trees and there is a fence directly ahead. Turn left. The narrow path suddenly broadens out and a bridge appears on the left.

11 Cross the bridge and walk straight ahead, until you reach a fence. Turn right and follow the path along the hedge. Horses may often be seen in this field. The path is a long one, following the sides of the field and eventually bears to the left.

12 At the road, turn left into **Fen Street**. There is no footpath. This is a narrow and very quiet country road.

13 Follow the road straight ahead, ignoring any turnings. It passes a line of poplar trees and a house with an unusual owl plaque on the wall.

14 Keep walking ahead, ignoring the road to your right. You then return to where you left the road at Point 7. Go straight on down the road.

15 At the next T junction, turn left onto the pavement. Walk down the street, past the almshouses built in 1860. The road leads onto the common, passing the **Post Office Stores** and the unusual **Rod Alley Pond**.

16 Cross the road and walk straight on.

17 At the entrance to **Old Buckenham High School**, turn right and follow the path back to the car park beside the **Ox and Plough** pub.

Pulham Market

Covering a variety of landscapes, this is a walk that is sure to keep both walker and dog entertained. There is lots to see and plenty of unusual smells to keep dogs busy. The ditches can be deep in places, and there are many rabbit holes.

Pulham Market is a picture postcard village, complete with whitewashed buildings, thatched houses and a large village green close to the church. Walking through the fields and country lanes seems a world away from the busy A140 only a few minutes drive to the west.

Apart from a few cars and farm vehicles, the lanes used in this walk are quiet and offer all year round walking opportunities. Part of the route is uphill, but it is not very evident until you turn around and look to see the road winding back away in the distance.

This is an agricultural area, with arable fields and some livestock such as cows and geese. It makes for an unusual walk, since if you look closely there are many reminders of the Second World War when the area was occupied by USAAF troops. This was part of the area known as Little America, where USAAF airfields housed large numbers of airmen and planes.

Once onto the fields, the path twists and turns, and careful attention needs to be kept to watch for the appropriate markers. The sound of geese can sometimes be heard across the fields.

Terrain

Paths vary between relatively smooth bark and grass; and rough field walking. In places it can get muddy, especially in winter.

Where to park

Beside the Falcon Pub/Pulham Memorial Hall in the centre of the village. **OS map:** Landranger 134 (GR 197862 / IP21 4SU).

How to get there

Pulham Market is just east of the A140 midway between Diss and Long Stratton. Turn off opposite the B1134 and follow the road to the village centre and Station Road where you will find the Falcon pub.

Nearest refreshments

The Falcon pub in Pulham Market is dog friendly and has a beer garden (☎ 01379 676815).

Dog factors

Distance: 4 miles.
Road walking: About half the walk is along quiet country lanes without pavements.
Livestock: Cattle and geese may be found in some fenced fields adjoining the walk.
Stiles: None.
Nearest Vets: Oakwood Veterinary Group, Oakwood House, Fuller Road, Harleston IP20 9EA. ☎ 01379 852146,
Linden House Veterinary Centre, 70 Mission Road, Diss IP22 4HX. ☎ 01379 651183.

The Walk

1 Leave the car park by the narrow path between the pub and village hall. Go through the white picket fence and walk straight ahead, taking the path between the houses.

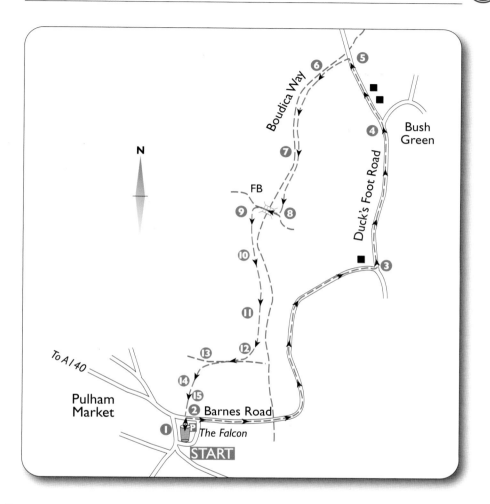

2 Turn right and follow the road out of the village. This is a quiet road without footpaths. There are tall hedges of beech, sycamore, oak and hawthorn on either side, opening out in places to give pleasant views across the surrounding countryside. The road winds uphill – but you do not realize this until you look back as it is quite a gentle gradient.

3 At the T junction, turn left into **Duck's Foot Road**. Follow the road onwards until you reach the next road junction marked **Bush Green/Hardwick**. Look out for the hardstanding on the right-hand side of the road, now used by farms to store crops and vehicles. In the Second World War this area was for aircraft.

4 Turn left and continue walking along **Duck's Foot Road**. The road passes several houses on the right-hand side, and goes down a little hill.

5 At the bottom of the hill, there is a line of poplar trees stretching out across the field to the left. Turn left into the field entrance. Ignore the little footbridge, and follow the path beside the poplar trees keeping the trees on your right.

6 The path leads alongside the edge of a field, often occupied by cows.

7 Eventually, the path curves to the left following a line of conifers. The conifers border a wildlife area that should not be entered. Keeping the conifers, then a ditch on your right, keep walking along the edge of the field.

8 Just before the corner of the field is reached, look for a turning on the right. This is marked by a **Boudicca Way** sign. Take this turning which leads through a tree lined tunnel, and across a sturdy boardwalk bridge.

9 At the end of the footbridge, turn left and follow the field path keeping the trees on your left as the field bends. Watch for a **Boudicca Way** sign on the left. Directly opposite the waymarker, the path leads straight across the field heading for the tree line opposite.

10 Take the path through the trees, over the footbridge and into the next field. Turn left and follow the path beside the deep ditch. This section of the path is quite long and goes between two fields, towards trees in the distance.

11 At the end of the field, there is a simple wooden footbridge of planks across a ditch, leading into the woodland. Follow the bark pathway through the wood.

12 Turn left at the end of the wood and follow the field path to your right. There will be a ditch on your left. At the end of the field, turn left following the line of the hedge. Keep walking straight ahead. **Pulham Market** can be seen in the distance.

13 At the left-hand corner of the field, cross the dyke and there is a **Boudicca Way** marker ahead. Turn left and follow the path.

14 A short distance up the field, turn right over the little bridge along a narrow corridor through the wood – again marked by a **Boudicca Way** marker. Take care as there are a number of exposed tree roots.

15 The path emerges onto a gravelled track leading past allotments and the bowls club. Follow the track down to the road. Cross the road, and walk up the path directly ahead past the 16th-century building '**the Old Bakery**' on your left, then through the alleyway and back to the car park.

Perfect walking weather.

Caistor St Edmund

Exploring Caistor St Edmund.

This is a walk with heritage in mind as well as quiet, wide open spaces offering lots of opportunities for exercising your pet. It is a very pretty walk, offering a variety of landscapes which are popular with dogs. The river is shallow and offers plenty of scope for splashing and playing, and with plenty to explore and lots of intriguing smells, the site is understandably irresistible to dog and owner!

The Roman site of Caistor St Edmund is a hidden town, unknown until the 20th century when a pilot spotted unusual lines in the earth. Excavations revealed that it was the site of the Roman town, 'Venta Icenorum'. The field edges and remains of the Roman walls still mark out the borders of the town, and during hot summers, the outlines of the roads may still be glimpsed.

This walk takes in sections of the walls, as well as cutting across fields that were used by the Romans as a site for houses and an amphitheatre. Saxon remains have also been found on the other side of the river.

Please check before entering a field as to whether there is any livestock present as sheep are used to keep the grass down across the site, and are moved around frequently. There are sometimes cows near the river. If there is no livestock in the fields, then dogs can safely be let off the leash.

Dog factors

Distance: 3 miles.
Road walking: None.
Livestock: Cattle and sheep may be in the fields, but they are rotated frequently and there are usually several fields left empty.
Stiles: None.
Nearest vets: Companion Care Vets, inside Pets at Home, Hall Road Retail Park, Hall Road, Norwich NR4 6DH. ☎ 01603 623040; Three Rivers Vets, The Veterinary Surgery, Norwich Road, Mulbarton NR14 8DE. ☎ 01508 570960

Terrain

Riverside, grass paths, some slopes and steps. It can get muddy after wet weather.

Where to park

Caistor Roman Town free car park. **OS map:** Landranger 134 Norwich and The Broads (GR 232033).

How to get there

Caistor St Edmund is 3 miles south of Norwich, near the A140. From the A140 turn off beside the Dunston Hall Hotel, follow the road to Stoke Holy Cross, turn left and then follow the road northwards.

Nearest refreshments

The Wildebeest Pub, on Norwich Road in Stoke Holy Cross serves food and has a large terrace outside where dogs are welcome (☎ 01508 492497).

The Walk

1 Leave the car park by the gate opposite the road. Walk straight ahead. This is a wide grassy path leading beside a raised embankment from where you can see the walls of the old **Roman town of Venta Icenorum**. Watch out for sheep in the adjacent field.

2 At the bottom of the field, walk straight across the field aiming for the bridge. Kissing gates give access to either end of the bridge. Ignore 2 kissing gates to the left of the bridge.

Norfolk – A Dog Walker's Guide

3 Cross the river and turn left, following the route of the river bank.

4 When the path begins to move away from the river, turn right and walk uphill across the field heading for the trees in the distance. This is quite a steep walk.

5 At the top of the ridge, turn right and follow the field line alongside the Norwich to London railway line, before curving round to the right past another field and down to the river bank. This field is extremely large, and if there is no livestock present it is a good site for letting dogs off the leash to have a run

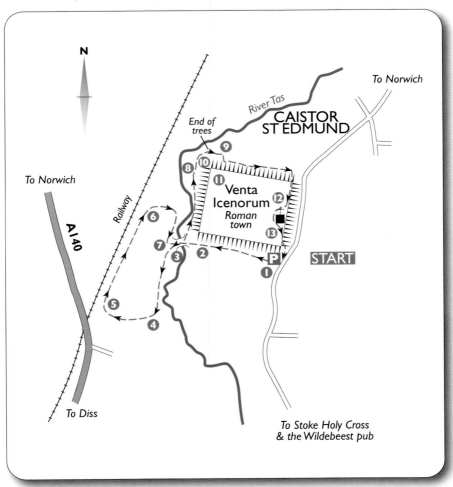

Crossing the River Tas.

and play. There are good views from the top of the field across the **Roman site** where the outline of the town can clearly be seen, as well as the adjacent field where it is known there were Roman houses and an amphitheatre.

6 Turn right to walk alongside the river and return to the bridge.

7 Cross the bridge, and turn left walking down to the next kissing gate. This passes a seat which is a lovely spot to relax on a summer's day. The river is quite shallow at this point and dogs always enjoy splashing through the water.

8 Go through the gate and continue to follow the river as it curves to the right.

9 At the end of the line of trees, turn slightly to your right and walk diagonally across the field towards another kissing gate. There are sometimes cows in this field.

10 Pass through the gate, turn right and through the next kissing gate. Walk up the bank in front of you. This is quite steep and can be a bit of a scramble for small dogs. It leads directly onto the wall walk. The path ends at another kissing gate. Go through the gate, then turn left and follow the path down the slope.

11 Go right along the path under the Roman wall to a flight of steps on the right. Climb the steps and follow the path on top of the wall towards the church. You could avoid the steps by going straight on then turning right along the path.

12 Go through the kissing gate to the church. This small church was partly built using recycled Roman tiles and bricks which you can spot at the bottom of the walls. Walk around the church to the right. Then walk diagonally across the churchyard to the gate on the far side.

13 Go through the gate and straight ahead. Take the first left hand turn which leads to a large chunk of Roman wall. At the bottom, turn right and walk towards a gate leading into the car park.

Lynford Stag and Thetford Forest

The Lyndford stag by the picnic area.

The rich smell of pine needles dominates this woodland walk! Thetford Forest is the largest lowland pine forest in Britain and is owned by the Forestry Commission. It was created after the First World War to provide new timber reserves. Pine plantations still dominate, but the increasing amount of traditional deciduous woodland being planted is creating a more varied image as the forest has diversified into leisure and tourism alongside conventional forestry.

This woodland walk is ideal for dog walkers who want an opportunity to socialize with other dogs they meet en route. You will usually encounter at least one or two other dog owners along the way. Dogs can be let off the leash for virtually all the walk, as only one minor road has to be crossed. There are plenty of wide spaces suitable for running and playing. Occasionally, the quiet of the wood is broken by the sound of jet aircraft from the nearby RAF/USAF airfield at Lakenheath. This can be startling to a dog unused to such sounds. Fortunately, the flights are not that frequent in general.

Planted on a grid system and interspersed with wide droves and smaller pathways, Thetford Forest is a pleasant place to walk. The old carriage drive to Lynford Hall forms part of the route of this walk. The woods are popular with dog walkers, as well as wildlife. If you are lucky, you might spot stone curlews, squirrels, golden pheasants, muntjac, roe and red deer while strolling through the forest. And despite being a very popular walking destination, the sheer size of the forest means that there is never any sense of being overwhelmed by other walkers.

There is a giant metal stag at the entrance to the picnic area which easily identifies the start of this walk. Forestry Commission workers discovered the sculpture when this area was being planted many years ago. Research identified the stag as having belonged to Sir Richard Sutton, the former owner of the nearby Lynford Hall. It seems he had been the Master of the Hunt locally and the sculpture was used as a practice target. If you look closely, the scars of its previous existence can still be seen! Nearby is a giant wooden play sculpture of a deer, which is popular with children in the summer.

Terrain
Flat, easy walking on grass and woodland pathways.

Where to park
This is easy to spot – look for the giant stag! Lots of parking available. **OS map:** Landranger 144 Thetford and Diss (GR 815916).

How to get there
From the A11 Thetford bypass turn onto the A134 Thetford/Downham Market road. Drive straight up the road, until you pass the signs for Grime's Graves on the left. The Lynford Stag parking area is a little further on, on the right-hand side of the road.

Nearest refreshments
There is a picnic site and a good range of pubs and cafés in Thetford.

Dog factors

Distance: 3.5 miles.
Road walking: One minor road has to be crossed and re-crossed.
Livestock: None.
Stiles: None.
Nearest vets: Eastgate Veterinary Group, 31 Bury Rd, Thetford, IP24 3AW. ☎ 01842 753991.

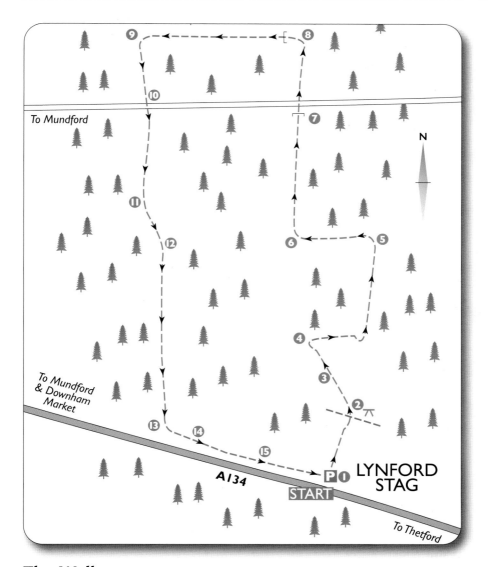

The Walk

1 Leave the car park by the grass path at the barrier near the metal stag sculpture.

Norfolk – A Dog Walker's Guide

2 Passing a bench on the right hand side of the path, walk directly ahead. Turn left just before reaching a picnic table.

3 Walk straight ahead, heading for the gap in the trees. This leads onto a short stretch of narrow grassy pathway, before entering a wide grassy drove.

4 Turn right onto the drove. Go past the green marker on the left hand side, and follow the path onwards as it winds to the left.

5 An 'unauthorized person sign' can be seen directly ahead. Turn left, and follow the wide pathway straight ahead. Green markers may be seen from time to time.

6 Just after passing a seat on the right hand side of the path, turn right. This path is very wide as it is one of the major routes through the forest. A long, straight grassy path, it leads through a pine plantation.

7 At the barrier, walk past the **white 37 marker** and cross the road. Re-enter the forest via the pathway beside a **white 34 marker**. Walk on.

8 Take the next turning to the left, past a black and yellow barrier. Walk carefully as the pathway is covered with rubble. Eventually the path becomes much more grassy. Keep walking straight ahead until you reach a T-junction.

9 Turn left, and walk down the wide pathway. This is a much firmer and well used path, leading back down to the road.

10 Cross over the road. Turn right and then take a sharp left to re-enter the forest at the **white 38 marker**. This is quite a wide grassy path.

11 At the next T-junction, turn left and walk straight on.

12 Take the next right hand turning which leads down a wide drove.

13 Turn left at the next turning, and you will shortly see a **blue marker** on your left hand side.

14 Walk straight ahead along a very wide, grassy path. The **Thetford/Downham Market** road can be glimpsed through the trees. The path curves slightly to the left as you walk along, before going horizontal to the road.

15 Keep walking ahead until you reach the car park again.

Burston

Beautiful blossom on a spring day.

The country lanes offer lots of potential smells and new experiences for inquisitive dogs! Although much of the walk is along country lanes, it is quite easy going as there are no gradients. Accessible all year round, this is a very pleasant walk for dog and owner. In springtime, the numerous orchards around the village are very pretty and full of blossom. Many of the apples are used to make cider.

The longest running strike in history combined with orchards and country lanes makes for an extremely unusual walk. This quiet village just north of Diss was the setting for a strike by schoolchildren lasting 25 years!

The strike began in 1914 when Tom and Kitty Higdon, the teachers at Burston School, were dismissed after complaining about poor conditions in the school, including inadequate heating, lighting and ventilation. On one occasion, the school managers had complained that Kitty Higdon had lit a fire without permission – she had done so to dry the clothes of children who had walked three miles to school in the rain. The day after they were dismissed, 66 of the school's 72 children went on strike in their support – and never returned to the school. Instead, Tom and Kitty Higdon continued to teach the children in a variety of locations, starting in a marquee on the Green, and eventually in the Burston Strike School, built in 1917 by public subscription including donations from several unions. The Higdon's defiance of the school authorities became an issue for trade unionists and school reformers throughout the country. The Strike School continued until 1939 when Tom Higdon died. Kitty was 75 years old by then and unable to continue teaching. The remaining 11 pupils moved to the Council School. An annual rally commemorating the strike is held every year on the first Sunday in September.

Terrain
Country lanes and field tracks.

Where to park
On the green beside Burston Strike School Museum. **OS map:** Landranger 144 Thetford and Diss (GR 137832).

How to get there
Burston is 3 miles north of Diss. Follow signs from Diss or leave the A140, east of Burston, at Dickleburgh Moor.

Nearest refreshments
The 16th-century Burston Crown, in the village, has a large beer garden and serves food every day except Mondays (☎ 01379 741257 / IP22 5TW).

Dog factors

Distance: 3 miles.
Road walking: About three quarters of the walk is via country lanes and village streets without pavements.
Livestock: No.
Stiles: 1.
Nearest vets: Linden House Veterinary Centre, 70 Mission Road, Diss IP22 4HX. ☎ 01379 651183; Uplands Way Vets Ltd., Diss IP22 4DF. ☎ 01379 642865.

The Walk

1 Return to the road and turn left, then left again just before the **Burston Crown**. This is a tarmaced road and there are no footpaths.

2 Walk up the road past the **Burston Chapel**. In springtime, the orchards on the right-hand side are a pretty sight as they are filled with apple blossom.

3 Just past the 30 mph road sign, turn left and take the path marked by a stile. Continue walking up the wide grassy path leading between a vineyard and apple orchards. It is a firm, easy to walk path. Go through the gate and turn right, then take the first left. This path leads between the trees. At the end of the path, there is a fence. Go through the gap in the trees which can be seen slightly to the left, and go straight ahead.

4 Turn left onto the grassy track.

5 A short distance down the trackway, there is a turning to the right into a field. Take this turning and walk along the edge of the field keeping the hedge on the right, passing a public footpath marker. This is an open field track. Keep walking along the track until you reach a road.

6 Turn right into **Back Lane**. This is a narrow, quiet lane used infrequently by cars and farm traffic.

7 At the T junction marked by a signpost, turn right following the road towards **Burston**. This is another very quiet lane known as **Hall Road** leading past fields and farms.

8 On entering the village, turn left at the post box into **Mill Green**. The road sign is not very evident until you actually turn. The road sign includes an unusual notice – 'The Higdons lived here until Tom died in 1939'. The route goes past a range of thatched cottages and white washed buildings. Passing the 40mph sign, the road leads into **Bridge Road** past open fields. On the left hand side of the road, behind the hedge there are a series of wooden railway carriages. Keep walking straight ahead, past **Grove Farm**.

9 At the T junction, turn right into **Bridge Lane**. There is a signpost marked Burston ¾ mile. A footpath appears towards the end of this road.

10 Turn right into **Station Road** and continue walking past the school. The road leads past the **Burston Crown** public house and back to the car park.

Burston Strike School is open all year for visitors.